DOVER·THRIFT·EDITIONS

Goblin Market and Other Poems

CHRISTINA ROSSETTI

DOVER PUBLICATIONS, INC.
New York

DOVER THRIFT EDITIONS
GENERAL EDITOR: STANLEY APPELBAUM
EDITOR OF THIS VOLUME: CANDACE WARD

Copyright

Copyright © 1994 by Dover Publications, Inc.
All rights reserved under Pan American and International Copyright Conventions.

Published in Canada by General Publishing Company, Ltd., 30 Lesmill Road, Don Mills, Toronto, Ontario.
Published in the United Kingdom by Constable and Company, Ltd., 3 The Lanchesters, 162–164 Fulham Palace Road, London W6 9ER.

Bibliographical Note

Goblin Market and Other Poems, first published in 1994 by Dover Publications, Inc., is a new selection of 53 poems reprinted from a standard text. The Note and alphabetical lists of titles and first lines have been specially prepared for this edition.

Library of Congress Cataloging-in-Publication Data

Rossetti, Christina Georgina, 1830–1894.
    Goblin market, and other poems / Christina Rossetti.
        p.   cm. — (Dover thrift editions)
    ISBN 0-486-28055-1 (pbk.)
    I. Title. II. Series.
PR5237.G6   1994
821'.8—dc20   93-40975
                                                                                                      CIP

Manufactured in the United States of America
Dover Publications, Inc., 31 East 2nd Street, Mineola, N.Y. 11501

Note

CHRISTINA GEORGINA ROSSETTI, born in 1830, was the youngest child of the Rossetti family. Her father was a Dante scholar who left Italy in protest of Austrian rule and her mother was an ex-governess of Anglo-Italian descent. With her brothers Dante Gabriel and William Michael, Christina grew up in an artistically rich household, encouraged to pursue her poetic inclinations. She contributed poetry to the Pre-Raphaelite magazine *The Germ*, but that movement's sensuousness contrasted to the explicitly religious aspects of her own artistic philosophy.

Despite Rossetti's intense involvement with the Anglo-Catholic movement of the Church of England, however, her poetry is rich in Pre-Raphaelite symbolism and sensuality, even in the devotional poems. Rossetti's first published collection, *Goblin Market and Other Poems* (1862), contains examples of such devotional pieces, and the complaint in "A Better Resurrection" exhibits the same passion as that found in such secular poems as "Echo" and "The Convent Threshold." Yet the intensity of her poetry often veiled a romantic melancholy that prompted Virginia Woolf to note, "Death, oblivion, and rest lap around your songs with their dark wave." As with many nineteenth-century women artists, this dark side of Rossetti's poetry seemed to reflect the austerity of her private life. Most of her adulthood was spent in relative seclusion, caring for invalid relations and doing charity work; she never married, twice turning down marriage proposals for religious reasons. Even so, Rossetti's poetic achievement is astounding and the beauty of her work is as provocative today as when it was first published over a hundred years ago.

Contents

From *Goblin Market and Other Poems*, 1862

Goblin Market	1
Dream Land	16
At Home	17
A Triad	18
Cousin Kate	19
Spring	20
A Birthday	21
Remember	22
After Death	22
An End	23
Song ("Oh roses for the flush of youth")	24
A Summer Wish	24
An Apple Gathering	25
Song ("Two doves upon the selfsame branch")	26
Maude Clare	26
Echo	28
Winter: My Secret	28
Another Spring	30
"No, Thank You, John"	30
May	32
A Pause of Thought	32
Song ("When I am dead, my dearest")	33

Sister Maude	33
The First Spring Day	34
The Convent Threshold	35
Up-Hill	39
"A Bruised Reed Shall He Not Break"	40
A Better Resurrection	40
The Three Enemies	41
The One Certainty	43
Sweet Death	44
The World	45

From *The Prince's Progress and Other Poems*, 1866

Spring Quiet	45
A Portrait	46
Dream-Love	47
Twice	49
One Day	51
A Dream	52
Beauty Is Vain	52
What Would I Give?	53
The Bourne	53
Memory	54
Shall I Forget?	55
Vanity of Vanities	55
L.E.L.	56
Life and Death	57
Grown and Flown	58
Despised and Rejected	59
The Lowest Place	60

From *Goblin Market, The Prince's Progress and Other Poems*, 1875

    Consider   61
    A Smile and a Sigh   62
    Paradise: In a Dream   62

From *New Poems, Hitherto Unpublished or Uncollected*, 1896

    Sleeping at Last   64

Goblin Market
and
Other Poems

Goblin Market

Morning and evening
Maids heard the goblins cry
"Come buy our orchard fruits,
Come buy, come buy:
Apples and quinces,
Lemons and oranges,
Plump unpecked cherries,
Melons and raspberries,
Bloom-down-cheeked peaches,
Swart-headed mulberries,
Wild free-born cranberries,
Crab-apples, dewberries,
Pine-apples, blackberries,
Apricots, strawberries; —
All ripe together
In summer weather, —
Morns that pass by,
Fair eves that fly;
Come buy, come buy:
Our grapes fresh from the vine,
Pomegranates full and fine,
Dates and sharp bullaces,
Rare pears and greengages,
Damsons and bilberries,
Taste them and try:
Currants and gooseberries,
Bright-fire-like barberries,
Figs to fill your mouth,
Citrons from the South,
Sweet to tongue and sound to eye;
Come buy, come buy."

   Evening by evening
Among the brookside rushes,
Laura bowed her head to hear,

Lizzie veiled her blushes:
Crouching close together
In the cooling weather,
With clasping arms and cautioning lips,
With tingling cheeks and finger tips.
"Lie close," Laura said,
Pricking up her golden head:
"We must not look at goblin men,
We must not buy their fruits:
Who knows upon what soil they fed
Their hungry thirsty roots?"
"Come buy," call the goblins
Hobbling down the glen.
"Oh," cried Lizzie, "Laura, Laura,
You should not peep at goblin men."
Lizzie covered up her eyes,
Covered close lest they should look;
Laura reared her glossy head,
And whispered like the restless brook:
"Look, Lizzie, look, Lizzie,
Down the glen tramp little men.
One hauls a basket,
One bears a plate,
One lugs a golden dish
Of many pounds weight.
How fair the vine must grow
Whose grapes are so luscious;
How warm the wind must blow
Through those fruit bushes."
"No," said Lizzie: "No, no, no;
Their offers should not charm us,
Their evil gifts would harm us."
She thrust a dimpled finger
In each ear, shut eyes and ran:
Curious Laura chose to linger
Wondering at each merchant man.
One had a cat's face,
One whisked a tail,

One tramped at a rat's pace,
One crawled like a snail,
One like a wombat prowled obtuse and furry,
One like a ratel tumbled hurry skurry.
She heard a voice like voice of doves
Cooing all together:
They sounded kind and full of loves
In the pleasant weather.

Laura stretched her gleaming neck
Like a rush-imbedded swan,
Like a lily from the beck,
Like a moonlit poplar branch,
Like a vessel at the launch
When its last restraint is gone.

Backwards up the mossy glen
Turned and trooped the goblin men,
With their shrill repeated cry,
"Come buy, come buy."
When they reached where Laura was
They stood stock still upon the moss,
Leering at each other,
Brother with queer brother;
Signalling each other,
Brother with sly brother.
One set his basket down,
One reared his plate;
One began to weave a crown
Of tendrils, leaves, and rough nuts brown
(Men sell not such in any town);
One heaved the golden weight
Of dish and fruit to offer her:
"Come buy, come buy," was still their cry.
Laura stared but did not stir,
Longed but had no money:
The whisk-tailed merchant bade her taste
In tones as smooth as honey,

The cat-faced purr'd,
The rat-paced spoke a word
Of welcome, and the snail-paced even was heard;
One parrot-voiced and jolly
Cried "Pretty Goblin" still for "Pretty Polly;"—
One whistled like a bird.

   But sweet-tooth Laura spoke in haste:
"Good folk, I have no coin;
To take were to purloin:
I have no copper in my purse,
I have no silver either,
And all my gold is on the furze
That shakes in windy weather
Above the rusty heather."
"You have much gold upon your head,"
They answered all together:
"Buy from us with a golden curl."
She clipped a precious golden lock,
She dropped a tear more rare than pearl,
Then sucked their fruit globes fair or red:
Sweeter than honey from the rock,
Stronger than man-rejoicing wine,
Clearer than water flowed that juice;
She never tasted such before,
How should it cloy with length of use?
She sucked and sucked and sucked the more
Fruits which that unknown orchard bore;
She sucked until her lips were sore;
Then flung the emptied rinds away
But gathered up one kernel-stone,
And knew not was it night or day
As she turned home alone.

   Lizzie met her at the gate
Full of wise upbraidings:
"Dear, you should not stay so late,
Twilight is not good for maidens;
Should not loiter in the glen

In the haunts of goblin men.
Do you not remember Jeanie,
How she met them in the moonlight,
Took their gifts both choice and many,
Ate their fruits and wore their flowers
Plucked from bowers
Where summer ripens at all hours?
But ever in the noonlight
She pined and pined away;
Sought them by night and day,
Found them no more, but dwindled and grew grey;
Then fell with the first snow,
While to this day no grass will grow
Where she lies low:
I planted daisies there a year ago
That never blow.
You should not loiter so."
"Nay, hush," said Laura:
"Nay, hush, my sister:
I ate and ate my fill,
Yet my mouth waters still;
To-morrow night I will
Buy more;" and kissed her:
"Have done with sorrow;
I'll bring you plums to-morrow
Fresh on their mother twigs,
Cherries worth getting;
You cannot think what figs
My teeth have met in,
What melons icy-cold
Piled on a dish of gold
Too huge for me to hold,
What peaches with a velvet nap,
Pellucid grapes without one seed:
Odorous indeed must be the mead
Whereon they grow, and pure the wave they drink
With lilies at the brink,
And sugar-sweet their sap."

    Golden head by golden head,
Like two pigeons in one nest
Folded in each other's wings,
They lay down in their curtained bed:
Like two blossoms on one stem,
Like two flakes of new-fall'n snow,
Like two wands of ivory
Tipped with gold for awful kings.
Moon and stars gazed in at them,
Wind sang to them lullaby,
Lumbering owls forbore to fly,
Not a bat flapped to and fro
Round their rest:
Cheek to cheek and breast to breast
Locked together in one nest.

    Early in the morning
When the first cock crowed his warning,
Neat like bees, as sweet and busy,
Laura rose with Lizzie:
Fetched in honey, milked the cows,
Aired and set to rights the house,
Kneaded cakes of whitest wheat,
Cakes for dainty mouths to eat,
Next churned butter, whipped up cream,
Fed their poultry, sat and sewed;
Talked as modest maidens should:
Lizzie with an open heart,
Laura in an absent dream,
One content, one sick in part;
One warbling for the mere bright day's delight,
One longing for the night.

    At length slow evening came:
They went with pitchers to the reedy brook;
Lizzie most placid in her look,
Laura most like a leaping flame.
They drew the gurgling water from its deep;
Lizzie plucked purple and rich golden flags,

Then turning homewards said: "The sunset flushes
Those furthest loftiest crags;
Come, Laura, not another maiden lags,
No wilful squirrel wags,
The beasts and birds are fast asleep."
But Laura loitered still among the rushes
And said the bank was steep.

And said the hour was early still,
The dew not fall'n, the wind not chill:
Listening ever, but not catching
The customary cry,
"Come buy, come buy,"
With its iterated jingle
Of sugar-baited words:
Not for all her watching
Once discerning even one goblin
Racing, whisking, tumbling, hobbling;
Let alone the herds
That used to tramp along the glen,
In groups or single,
Of brisk fruit-merchant men.

Till Lizzie urged, "O Laura, come;
I hear the fruit-call, but I dare not look:
You should not loiter longer at this brook:
Come with me home.
The stars rise, the moon bends her arc,
Each glowworm winks her spark,
Let us get home before the night grows dark:
For clouds may gather
Though this is summer weather,
Put out the lights and drench us through;
Then if we lost our way what should we do?"

Laura turned cold as stone
To find her sister heard that cry alone,
That goblin cry,
"Come buy our fruits, come buy."

Must she then buy no more such dainty fruit?
Must she no more such succous pasture find,
Gone deaf and blind?
Her tree of life drooped from the root:
She said not one word in her heart's sore ache;
But peering thro' the dimness, nought discerning,
Trudged home, her pitcher dripping all the way;
So crept to bed, and lay
Silent till Lizzie slept;
Then sat up in a passionate yearning,
And gnashed her teeth for baulked desire, and wept
As if her heart would break.

   Day after day, night after night,
Laura kept watch in vain
In sullen silence of exceeding pain.
She never caught again the goblin cry:
"Come buy, come buy;" —
She never spied the goblin men
Hawking their fruits along the glen:
But when the noon waxed bright
Her hair grew thin and grey;
She dwindled, as the fair full moon doth turn
To swift decay and burn
Her fire away.

   One day remembering her kernel-stone
She set it by a wall that faced the south;
Dewed it with tears, hoped for a root.
Watched for a waxing shoot,
But there came none;
It never saw the sun,
It never felt the trickling moisture run:
While with sunk eyes and faded mouth
She dreamed of melons, as a traveller sees
False waves in desert drouth
With shade of leaf-crowned trees,
And burns the thirstier in the sandful breeze.

She no more swept the house,
Tended the fowls or cows,
Fetched honey, kneaded cakes of wheat,
Brought water from the brook:
But sat down listless in the chimney-nook
And would not eat.

Tender Lizzie could not bear
To watch her sister's cankerous care
Yet not to share.
She night and morning
Caught the goblins' cry:
"Come buy our orchard fruits,
Come buy, come buy:" —
Beside the brook, along the glen,
She heard the tramp of goblin men,
The voice and stir
Poor Laura could not hear;
Longed to buy fruit to comfort her,
But feared to pay too dear.
She thought of Jeanie in her grave,
Who should have been a bride;
But who for joys brides hope to have
Fell sick and died
In her gay prime,
In earliest Winter time,
With the first glazing rime,
With the first snow-fall of crisp Winter time.

Till Laura dwindling
Seemed knocking at Death's door:
Then Lizzie weighed no more
Better and worse;
But put a silver penny in her purse,
Kissed Laura, crossed the heath with clumps of furze
At twilight, halted by the brook:
And for the first time in her life
Began to listen and look.

Laughed every goblin
When they spied her peeping:
Came towards her hobbling,
Flying, running, leaping,
Puffing and blowing,
Chuckling, clapping, crowing,
Clucking and gobbling,
Mopping and mowing,
Full of airs and graces,
Pulling wry faces,
Demure grimaces,
Cat-like and rat-like,
Ratel- and wombat-like,
Snail-paced in a hurry,
Parrot-voiced and whistler,
Helter skelter, hurry skurry,
Chattering like magpies,
Fluttering like pigeons,
Gliding like fishes,—
Hugged her and kissed her:
Squeezed and caressed her:
Stretched up their dishes,
Panniers, and plates:
"Look at our apples
Russet and dun,
Bob at our cherries,
Bite at our peaches,
Citrons and dates,
Grapes for the asking,
Pears red with basking
Out in the sun,
Plums on their twigs;
Pluck them and suck them,
Pomegranates, figs."—

"Good folk," said Lizzie,
Mindful of Jeanie:
"Give me much and many:"—

Held out her apron,
Tossed them her penny.
"Nay, take a seat with us,
Honour and eat with us,"
They answered grinning:
"Our feast is but beginning,
Night yet is early,
Warm and dew-pearly,
Wakeful and starry:
Such fruits as these
No man can carry;
Half their bloom would fly,
Half their dew would dry,
Half their flavour would pass by.
Sit down and feast with us,
Be welcome guest with us,
Cheer you and rest with us." —
"Thank you," said Lizzie: "But one waits
At home alone for me:
So without further parleying,
If you will not sell me any
Of your fruits though much and many,
Give me back my silver penny
I tossed you for a fee." —
They began to scratch their pates,
No longer wagging, purring,
But visibly demurring,
Grunting and snarling.
One called her proud,
Cross-grained, uncivil;
Their tones waxed loud,
Their looks were evil.
Lashing their tails
They trod and hustled her,
Elbowed and jostled her,
Clawed with their nails,
Barking, mewing, hissing, mocking,
Tore her gown and soiled her stocking,

Twitched her hair out by the roots,
Stamped upon her tender feet,
Held her hands and squeezed their fruits
Against her mouth to make her eat.

    White and golden Lizzie stood,
Like a lily in a flood, —
Like a rock of blue-veined stone
Lashed by tides obstreperously, —
Like a beacon left alone
In a hoary roaring sea,
Sending up a golden fire, —
Like a fruit-crowned orange-tree
White with blossoms honey-sweet
Sore beset by wasp and bee, —
Like a royal virgin town
Topped with gilded dome and spire
Close beleaguered by a fleet
Mad to tug her standard down.

    One may lead a horse to water,
Twenty cannot make him drink.
Though the goblins cuffed and caught her,
Coaxed and fought her,
Bullied and besought her,
Scratched her, pinched her black as ink,
Kicked and knocked her,
Mauled and mocked her,
Lizzie uttered not a word;
Would not open lip from lip
Lest they should cram a mouthful in:
But laughed in heart to feel the drip
Of juice that syrupped all her face,
And lodged in dimples of her chin,
And streaked her neck which quaked like curd.
At last the evil people,
Worn out by her resistance,
Flung back her penny, kicked their fruit
Along whichever road they took,

Not leaving root or stone or shoot;
Some writhed into the ground,
Some dived into the brook
With ring and ripple,
Some scudded on the gale without a sound,
Some vanished in the distance.

　In a smart, ache, tingle,
Lizzie went her way;
Knew not was it night or day;
Sprang up the bank, tore thro' the furze,
Threaded copse and dingle,
And heard her penny jingle
Bouncing in her purse, —
Its bounce was music to her ear.
She ran and ran
As if she feared some goblin man
Dogged her with gibe or curse
Or something worse:
But not one goblin skurried after,
Nor was she pricked by fear;
The kind heart made her windy-paced
That urged her home quite out of breath with haste
And inward laughter.

　She cried "Laura," up the garden,
"Did you miss me?
Come and kiss me.
Never mind my bruises,
Hug me, kiss me, suck my juices
Squeezed from goblin fruits for you,
Goblin pulp and goblin dew.
Eat me, drink me, love me;
Laura, make much of me;
For your sake I have braved the glen
And had to do with goblin merchant men."

　Laura started from her chair,
Flung her arms up in the air,

Clutched her hair:
"Lizzie, Lizzie, have you tasted
For my sake the fruit forbidden?
Must your light like mine be hidden,
Your young life like mine be wasted,
Undone in mine undoing,
And ruined in my ruin,
Thirsty, cankered, goblin-ridden?" —
She clung about her sister,
Kissed and kissed and kissed her:
Tears once again
Refreshed her shrunken eyes,
Dropping like rain
After long sultry drouth;
Shaking with aguish fear, and pain,
She kissed and kissed her with a hungry mouth.

    Her lips began to scorch,
That juice was wormwood to her tongue,
She loathed the feast:
Writhing as one possessed she leaped and sung,
Rent all her robe, and wrung
Her hands in lamentable haste,
And beat her breast.
Her locks streamed like the torch
Borne by a racer at full speed,
Or like the mane of horses in their flight,
Or like an eagle when she stems the light
Straight toward the sun,
Or like a caged thing freed,
Or like a flying flag when armies run.

    Swift fire spread through her veins, knocked at her heart,
Met the fire smouldering there
And overbore its lesser flame;
She gorged on bitterness without a name:
Ah! fool, to choose such part
Of soul-consuming care!
Sense failed in the mortal strife:

Like the watch-tower of a town
Which an earthquake shatters down,
Like a lightning-stricken mast,
Like a wind-uprooted tree
Spun about,
Like a foam-topped waterspout
Cast down headlong in the sea,
She fell at last;
Pleasure past and anguish past,
Is it death or is it life?

   Life out of death.
That night long Lizzie watched by her,
Counted her pulse's flagging stir,
Felt for her breath,
Held water to her lips, and cooled her face
With tears and fanning leaves:
But when the first birds chirped about their eaves,
And early reapers plodded to the place
Of golden sheaves,
And dew-wet grass
Bowed in the morning winds so brisk to pass,
And new buds with new day
Opened of cup-like lilies on the stream,
Laura awoke as from a dream,
Laughed in the innocent old way,
Hugged Lizzie but not twice or thrice;
Her gleaming locks showed not one thread of grey
Her breath was sweet as May
And light danced in her eyes.

   Days, weeks, months, years
Afterwards, when both were wives
With children of their own;
Their mother-hearts beset with fears,
Their lives bound up in tender lives;
Laura would call the little ones
And tell them of her early prime,
Those pleasant days long gone

Of not-returning time:
Would talk about the haunted glen,
The wicked, quaint fruit-merchant men,
Their fruits like honey to the throat
But poison in the blood;
(Men sell not such in any town):
Would tell them how her sister stood
In deadly peril to do her good,
And win the fiery antidote:
Then joining hands to little hands
Would bid them cling together,
"For there is no friend like a sister
In calm or stormy weather;
To cheer one on the tedious way,
To fetch one if one goes astray,
To lift one if one totters down,
To strengthen whilst one stands."

Dream Land

Where sunless rivers weep
Their waves into the deep,
She sleeps a charmèd sleep:
   Awake her not.
Led by a single star,
She came from very far
To seek where shadows are
   Her pleasant lot.

She left the rosy morn,
She left the fields of corn,
For twilight cold and lorn
   And water springs.
Through sleep, as through a veil,
She sees the sky look pale,
And hears the nightingale
   That sadly sings.

Rest, rest, a perfect rest
Shed over brow and breast;
Her face is toward the west,
   The purple land.
She cannot see the grain
Ripening on hill and plain;
She cannot feel the rain
   Upon her hand.

Rest, rest, for evermore
Upon a mossy shore;
Rest, rest at the heart's core
   Till time shall cease:
Sleep that no pain shall wake,
Night that no morn shall break
Till joy shall overtake
   Her perfect peace.

At Home

When I was dead, my spirit turned
   To seek the much-frequented house:
I passed the door, and saw my friends
   Feasting beneath the green orange boughs;
From hand to hand they pushed the wine,
   They sucked the pulp of plum and peach;
They sang, they jested, and they laughed,
   For each was loved of each.

I listened to their honest chat:
   Said one: "To-morrow we shall be
Plod plod along the featureless sands
   And coasting miles and miles of sea."
Said one: "Before the turn of tide
   We will achieve the eyrie-seat."
Said one: "To-morrow shall be like
   To-day, but much more sweet."

"To-morrow," said they, strong with hope,
   And dwelt upon the pleasant way:
"To-morrow," cried they one and all,
   While no one spoke of yesterday.
Their life stood full at blessed noon;
   I, only I, had passed away:
"To-morrow and to-day," they cried;
   I was of yesterday.

I shivered comfortless, but cast
   No chill across the tablecloth;
I all-forgotten shivered, sad
   To stay and yet to part how loth:
I passed from the familiar room,
   I who from love had passed away,
Like the remembrance of a guest
   That tarrieth but a day.

A Triad

SONNET

Three sang of love together: one with lips
   Crimson, with cheeks and bosom in a glow,
Flushed to the yellow hair and finger-tips;
   And one there sang who soft and smooth as snow
   Bloomed like a tinted hyacinth at a show;
And one was blue with famine after love,
   Who like a harpstring snapped rang harsh and low
The burden of what those were singing of.
One shamed herself in love; one temperately
   Grew gross in soulless love, a sluggish wife;
One famished died for love. Thus two of three
   Took death for love and won him after strife;
One droned in sweetness like a fattened bee:
   All on the threshold, yet all short of life.

Cousin Kate

I was a cottage maiden
   Hardened by sun and air,
Contented with my cottage mates,
   Not mindful I was fair.
Why did a great lord find me out,
   And praise my flaxen hair?
Why did a great lord find me out
   To fill my heart with care?

He lured me to his palace home—
   Woe's me for joy thereof—
To lead a shameless shameful life,
   His plaything and his love.
He wore me like a silken knot,
   He changed me like a glove;
So now I moan, an unclean thing,
   Who might have been a dove.

O Lady Kate, my cousin Kate,
   You grew more fair than I:
He saw you at your father's gate,
   Chose you, and cast me by.
He watched your steps along the lane,
   Your work among the rye;
He lifted you from mean estate
   To sit with him on high.

Because you were so good and pure
   He bound you with his ring:
The neighbours call you good and pure,
   Call me an outcast thing.
Even so I sit and howl in dust,
   You sit in gold and sing:
Now which of us has tenderer heart?
   You had the stronger wing.

O cousin Kate, my love was true,
   Your love was writ in sand:
If he had fooled not me but you,
   If you stood where I stand,
He'd not have won me with his love
   Nor bought me with his land;
I would have spit into his face
   And not have taken his hand.

Yet I've a gift you have not got,
   And seem not like to get:
For all your clothes and wedding-ring
   I've little doubt you fret.
My fair-haired son, my shame, my pride,
   Cling closer, closer yet:
Your father would give lands for one
   To wear his coronet.

Spring

Frost-locked all the winter,
Seeds, and roots, and stones of fruits,
What shall make their sap ascend
That they may put forth shoots?
Tips of tender green,
Leaf, or blade, or sheath;
Telling of the hidden life
That breaks forth underneath,
Life nursed in its grave by Death.

Blows the thaw-wind pleasantly,
Drips the soaking rain,
By fits looks down the waking sun:
Young grass springs on the plain;
Young leaves clothe early hedgerow trees;
Seeds, and roots, and stones of fruits,

Swollen with sap put forth their shoots;
Curled-headed ferns sprout in the lane;
Birds sing and pair again.

There is no time like Spring,
When life's alive in everything,
Before new nestlings sing,
Before cleft swallows speed their journey back
Along the trackless track —
God guides their wing,
He spreads their table that they nothing lack, —
Before the daisy grows a common flower,
Before the sun has power
To scorch the world up in his noontide hour.

There is no time like Spring,
Like Spring that passes by:
There is no life like Spring-life born to die, —
Piercing the sod,
Clothing the uncouth clod,
Hatched in the nest,
Fledged on the windy bough,
Strong on the wing;
There is no time like Spring that passes by,
Now newly born, and now
Hastening to die.

A Birthday

My heart is like a singing bird
   Whose nest is in a watered shoot;
My heart is like an apple-tree
   Whose boughs are bent with thick-set fruit;
My heart is like a rainbow shell
   That paddles in a halcyon sea;
My heart is gladder than all these
   Because my love is come to me.

Raise me a dais of silk and down;
    Hang it with vair and purple dyes;
Carve it in doves, and pomegranates,
    And peacocks with a hundred eyes;
Work it in gold and silver grapes,
    In leaves, and silver fleurs-de-lys;
Because the birthday of my life
    Is come, my love is come to me.

Remember

SONNET

Remember me when I am gone away,
    Gone far away into the silent land;
    When you can no more hold me by the hand,
Nor I half turn to go yet turning stay.
Remember me when no more day by day
    You tell me of our future that you planned:
    Only remember me; you understand
It will be late to counsel then or pray.
Yet if you should forget me for a while
    And afterwards remember, do not grieve:
    For if the darkness and corruption leave
    A vestige of the thoughts that once I had,
Better by far you should forget and smile
    Than that you should remember and be sad.

After Death

SONNET

The curtains were half drawn, the floor was swept
    And strewn with rushes, rosemary and may
    Lay thick upon the bed on which I lay,

Where through the lattice ivy-shadows crept.
He leaned above me, thinking that I slept
   And could not hear him; but I heard him say:
   "Poor child, poor child:" and as he turned away
Came a deep silence, and I knew he wept.
He did not touch the shroud, or raise the fold
   That hid my face, or take my hand in his,
     Or ruffle the smooth pillows for my head:
       He did not love me living; but once dead
   He pitied me; and very sweet it is
To know he still is warm though I am cold.

An End

Love, strong as Death, is dead.
Come, let us make his bed
Among the dying flowers:
A green turf at his head;
And a stone at his feet,
Whereon we may sit
In the quiet evening hours.

He was born in the Spring,
And died before the harvesting:
On the last warm summer day
He left us; he would not stay
For Autumn twilight cold and grey.
Sit we by his grave, and sing
He is gone away.

To few chords and sad and low
Sing we so:
Be our eyes fixed on the grass
Shadow-veiled as the years pass
While we think of all that was
In the long ago.

Song

Oh roses for the flush of youth,
    And laurel for the perfect prime;
But pluck an ivy branch for me
    Grown old before my time.

Oh violets for the grave of youth,
    And bay for those dead in their prime;
Give me the withered leaves I chose
    Before in the old time.

A Summer Wish

Live all thy sweet life thro',
    Sweet Rose, dew-sprent,
Drop down thine evening dew
To gather it anew
When day is bright:
    I fancy thou wast meant
Chiefly to give delight.

Sing in the silent sky,
    Glad soaring bird;
Sing out thy notes on high
To sunbeam straying by
Or passing cloud;
    Heedless if thou art heard
Sing thy full song aloud.

Oh that it were with me
    As with the flower;
Blooming on its own tree
For butterfly and bee
Its summer morns:

That I might bloom mine hour
A rose in spite of thorns.

Oh that my work were done
   As birds' that soar
Rejoicing in the sun:
That when my time is run
And daylight too,
   I so might rest once more
Cool with refreshing dew.

An Apple Gathering

I plucked pink blossoms from mine apple-tree
   And wore them all that evening in my hair:
Then in due season when I went to see
   I found no apples there.

With dangling basket all along the grass
   As I had come I went the selfsame track:
My neighbours mocked me while they saw me pass
   So empty-handed back.

Lilian and Lilias smiled in trudging by,
   Their heaped-up basket teased me like a jeer;
Sweet-voiced they sang beneath the sunset sky,
   Their mother's home was near.

Plump Gertrude passed me with her basket full,
   A stronger hand than hers helped it along;
A voice talked with her through the shadows cool
   More sweet to me than song.

Ah Willie, Willie, was my love less worth
   Than apples with their green leaves piled above?
I counted rosiest apples on the earth
   Of far less worth than love.

So once it was with me you stooped to talk
    Laughing and listening in this very lane:
To think that by this way we used to walk
    We shall not walk again!

I let my neighbours pass me, ones and twos
    And groups; the latest said the night grew chill,
And hastened: but I loitered, while the dews
    Fell fast I loitered still.

Song

Two doves upon the selfsame branch,
    Two lilies on a single stem,
Two butterflies upon one flower: —
    Oh happy they who look on them.

Who look upon them hand in hand
    Flushed in the rosy summer light;
Who look upon them hand in hand
    And never give a thought to night.

Maude Clare

Out of the church she followed them
    With a lofty step and mien:
His bride was like a village maid,
    Maude Clare was like a queen.

"Son Thomas," his lady mother said,
    With smiles, almost with tears:
"May Nell and you but live as true
    As we have done for years;

"Your father thirty years ago
    Had just your tale to tell;

But he was not so pale as you,
   Nor I so pale as Nell."

My lord was pale with inward strife,
   And Nell was pale with pride;
My lord gazed long on pale Maude Clare
   Or ever he kissed the bride.

"Lo, I have brought my gift, my lord,
   Have brought my gift," she said:
"To bless the hearth, to bless the board,
   To bless the marriage-bed.

"Here's my half of the golden chain
   You wore about your neck,
That day we waded ankle-deep
   For lilies in the beck:

"Here's my half of the faded leaves
   We plucked from budding bough,
With feet amongst the lily leaves,—
   The lilies are budding now."

He strove to match her scorn with scorn,
   He faltered in his place:
"Lady," he said,—"Maude Clare," he said,—
   "Maude Clare:"—and hid his face.

She turn'd to Nell: "My Lady Nell,
   I have a gift for you;
Though, were it fruit, the bloom were gone,
   Or, were it flowers, the dew.

"Take my share of a fickle heart,
   Mine of a paltry love:
Take it or leave it as you will,
   I wash my hands thereof."

"And what you leave," said Nell, "I'll take,
   And what you spurn, I'll wear;

For he's my lord for better and worse,
    And him I love, Maude Clare.

"Yea, though you're taller by the head,
    More wise and much more fair;
I'll love him till he loves me best,
    Me best of all, Maude Clare."

Echo

Come to me in the silence of the night;
    Come in the speaking silence of a dream:
Come with soft rounded cheeks and eyes as bright
    As sunlight on a stream;
        Come back in tears,
O memory, hope, love of finished years.

Oh dream how sweet, too sweet, too bitter sweet,
    Whose wakening should have been in Paradise,
Where souls brimfull of love abide and meet;
    Where thirsting longing eyes
        Watch the slow door
That opening, letting in, lets out no more.

Yet come to me in dreams, that I may live
    My very life again though cold in death:
Come back to me in dreams, that I may give
    Pulse for pulse, breath for breath:
        Speak low, lean low,
As long ago, my love, how long ago!

Winter: My Secret

I tell my secret? No indeed, not I:
Perhaps some day, who knows?
But not today; it froze, and blows, and snows,

Winter: My Secret

And you're too curious: fie!
You want to hear it? well:
Only, my secret's mine, and I won't tell.

Or, after all, perhaps there's none:
Suppose there is no secret after all,
But only just my fun.
Today's a nipping day, a biting day;
In which one wants a shawl,
A veil, a cloak, and other wraps:
I cannot ope to every one who taps,
And let the draughts come whistling thro' my hall;
Come bounding and surrounding me,
Come buffeting, astounding me,
Nipping and clipping thro' my wraps and all.
I wear my mask for warmth: who ever shows
His nose to Russian snows
To be pecked at by every wind that blows?
You would not peck? I thank you for good will,
Believe, but leave that truth untested still.

Spring's an expansive time: yet I don't trust
March with its peck of dust,
Nor April with its rainbow-crowned brief showers,
Nor even May, whose flowers
One frost may wither thro' the sunless hours.

Perhaps some languid summer day,
When drowsy birds sing less and less,
And golden fruit is ripening to excess,
If there's not too much sun nor too much cloud,
And the warm wind is neither still nor loud,
Perhaps my secret I may say,
Or you may guess.

Another Spring

If I might see another Spring
   I'd not plant summer flowers and wait:
I'd have my crocuses at once,
My leafless pink mezereons,
   My chill-veined snowdrops, choicer yet
   My white or azure violet,
Leaf-nested primrose; anything
   To blow at once not late.

If I might see another Spring
   I'd listen to the daylight birds
That build their nests and pair and sing,
Nor wait for mateless nightingale;
   I'd listen to the lusty herds,
   The ewes with lambs as white as snow,
I'd find out music in the hail
   And all the winds that blow.

If I might see another Spring—
   Oh stinging comment on my past
That all my past results in "if"—
   If I might see another Spring
I'd laugh to-day, to-day is brief;
I would not wait for anything:
   I'd use to-day that cannot last,
   Be glad to-day and sing.

"No, Thank You, John"

I never said I loved you, John:
   Why will you tease me day by day,
And wax a weariness to think upon
     With always "do" and "pray"?

You know I never loved you, John;
    No fault of mine made me your toast:
Why will you haunt me with a face as wan
    As shows an hour-old ghost?

I dare say Meg or Moll would take
    Pity upon you, if you'd ask:
And pray don't remain single for my sake
    Who can't perform that task.

I have no heart? — Perhaps I have not;
    But then you're mad to take offence
That I don't give you what I have not got:
    Use your own common sense.

Let bygones be bygones:
    Don't call me false, who owed not to be true:
I'd rather answer "No" to fifty Johns
    Than answer "Yes" to you.

Let's mar our pleasant days no more,
    Song-birds of passage, days of youth:
Catch at today, forget the days before:
    I'll wink at your untruth.

Let us strike hands as hearty friends;
    No more, no less; and friendship's good:
Only don't keep in view ulterior ends,
    And points not understood

In open treaty. Rise above
    Quibbles and shuffling off and on:
Here's friendship for you if you like; but love, —
    No, thank you, John.

May

I cannot tell you how it was;
But this I know: it came to pass
Upon a bright and breezy day
When May was young; ah, pleasant May!
As yet the poppies were not born
Between the blades of tender corn;
The last eggs had not hatched as yet,
Nor any bird forgone its mate.

I cannot tell you what it was;
But this I know: it did but pass.
It passed away with sunny May,
With all sweet things it passed away,
And left me old, and cold, and grey.

A Pause of Thought

I looked for that which is not, nor can be,
   And hope deferred made my heart sick in truth:
   But years must pass before a hope of youth
     Is resigned utterly.

I watched and waited with a steadfast will:
   And though the object seemed to flee away
   That I so longed for, ever day by day
     I watched and waited still.

Sometimes I said: This thing shall be no more;
   My expectation wearies and shall cease;
   I will resign it now and be at peace:
     Yet never gave it o'er.

Sometimes I said: It is an empty name
   I long for; to a name why should I give

The peace of all the days I have to live? —
   Yet gave it all the same.

Alas, thou foolish one! alike unfit
   For healthy joy and salutary pain:
   Thou knowest the chase useless, and again
      Turnest to follow it.

Song

When I am dead, my dearest,
   Sing no sad songs for me;
Plant thou no roses at my head,
   Nor shady cypress tree:
Be the green grass above me
   With showers and dewdrops wet;
And if thou wilt, remember,
   And if thou wilt, forget.

I shall not see the shadows,
   I shall not feel the rain;
I shall not hear the nightingale
   Sing on, as if in pain:
And dreaming through the twilight
   That doth not rise nor set,
Haply I may remember,
   And haply may forget.

Sister Maude

Who told my mother of my shame,
   Who told my father of my dear?
Oh who but Maude, my sister Maude,
   Who lurked to spy and peer.

Cold he lies, as cold as stone,
    With his clotted curls about his face:
The comeliest corpse in all the world
    And worthy of a queen's embrace.

You might have spared his soul, sister,
    Have spared my soul, your own soul too:
Though I had not been born at all,
    He'd never have looked at you.

My father may sleep in Paradise,
    My mother at Heaven-gate:
But sister Maude shall get no sleep
    Either early or late.

My father may wear a golden gown,
    My mother a crown may win;
If my dear and I knocked at Heaven-gate
    Perhaps they'd let us in:
But sister Maude, oh sister Maude,
    Bide *you* with death and sin.

The First Spring Day

I wonder if the sap is stirring yet,
If wintry birds are dreaming of a mate,
If frozen snowdrops feel as yet the sun
And crocus fires are kindling one by one:
    Sing, robin, sing;
I still am sore in doubt concerning Spring.

I wonder if the springtide of this year
Will bring another Spring both lost and dear;
If heart and spirit will find out their Spring,
Or if the world alone will bud and sing:
    Sing, hope, to me;
Sweet notes, my hope, soft notes for memory.

The sap will surely quicken soon or late,
The tardiest bird will twitter to a mate;
So Spring must dawn again with warmth and bloom,
Or in this world, or in the world to come:
    Sing, voice of Spring,
Till I too blossom and rejoice and sing.

The Convent Threshold

There's blood between us, love, my love,
There's father's blood, there's brother's blood;
And blood's a bar I cannot pass:
I choose the stairs that mount above,
Stair after golden skyward stair,
To city and to sea of glass.
My lily feet are soiled with mud,
With scarlet mud which tells a tale
Of hope that was, of guilt that was,
Of love that shall not yet avail;
Alas, my heart, if I could bare
My heart, this selfsame stain is there:
I seek the sea of glass and fire
To wash the spot, to burn the snare;
Lo, stairs are meant to lift us higher:
Mount with me, mount the kindled stair.

Your eyes look earthward, mine look up.
I see the far-off city grand,
Beyond the hills a watered land,
Beyond the gulf a gleaming strand
Of mansions where the righteous sup;
Who sleep at ease among their trees,
Or wake to sing a cadenced hymn
With Cherubim and Seraphim;
They bore the Cross, they drained the cup,
Racked, roasted, crushed, wrenched limb from limb,

They the offscouring of the world:
The heaven of starry heavens unfurled,
The sun before their face is dim.

You looking earthward what see you?
Milk-white wine-flushed among the vines,
Up and down leaping, to and fro,
Most glad, most full, made strong with wines,
Blooming as peaches pearled with dew,
Their golden windy hair afloat,
Love-music warbling in their throat,
Young men and women come and go.

You linger, yet the time is short:
Flee for your life, gird up your strength
To flee; the shadows stretched at length
Show that day wanes, that night draws nigh;
Flee to the mountain, tarry not.
Is this a time for smile and sigh,
For songs among the secret trees
Where sudden blue birds nest and sport?
The time is short and yet you stay:
To-day while it is called to-day
Kneel, wrestle, knock, do violence, pray;
To-day is short, to-morrow nigh:
Why will you die? why will you die?

You sinned with me a pleasant sin:
Repent with me, for I repent.
Woe's me the lore I must unlearn!
Woe's me that easy way we went,
So rugged when I would return!
How long until my sleep begin,
How long shall stretch these nights and days?
Surely, clean Angels cry, she prays;
She laves her soul with tedious tears:
How long must stretch these years and years?
I turn from you my cheeks and eyes,

My hair which you shall see no more—
Alas for joy that went before,
For joy that dies, for love that dies.
Only my lips still turn to you,
My livid lips that cry, Repent.
Oh weary life, oh weary Lent,
Oh weary time whose stars are few.

How should I rest in Paradise,
Or sit on steps of heaven alone?
If Saints and Angels spoke of love
Should I not answer from my throne:
Have pity upon me, ye my friends,
For I have heard the sound thereof:
Should I not turn with yearning eyes,
Turn earthwards with a pitiful pang?
Oh save me from a pang in heaven.
By all the gifts we took and gave,
Repent, repent, and be forgiven:
This life is long, but yet it ends;
Repent and purge your soul and save:
No gladder song the morning stars
Upon their birthday morning sang
Than Angels sing when one repents.

I tell you what I dreamed last night:
A spirit with transfigured face
Fire-footed clomb an infinite space.
I heard his hundred pinions clang,
Heaven-bells rejoicing rang and rang,
Heaven-air was thrilled with subtle scents
Worlds spun upon their rushing cars:
He mounted shrieking: "Give me light."
Still light was poured on him, more light;
Angels, Archangels he outstripped
Exultant in exceeding might,
And trod the skirts of Cherubim.
Still "Give me light," he shrieked; and dipped

His thirsty face, and drank a sea,
Athirst with thirst it could not slake.
I saw him, drunk with knowledge, take
From aching brows the aureole crown —
His locks writhed like a cloven snake —
He left his throne to grovel down
And lick the dust of Seraph's feet:
For what is knowledge duly weighed?
Knowledge is strong but love is sweet;
Yea all the progress ye had made
Was but to learn that all is small
Save love, for love is all in all.

I tell you what I dreamed last night:
It was not dark, it was not light,
Cold dews had drenched my plenteous hair
Through clay; you came to seek me there.
And "Do you dream of me?" you said.
My heart was dust that used to leap
To you; I answered half asleep:
"My pillow is damp, my sheets are red,
There's a leaden tester to my bed:
Find you a warmer playfellow,
A warmer pillow for your head,
A kinder love to love than mine."
You wrung your hands; while I like lead
Crushed downwards through the sodden earth:
You smote your hands but not in mirth,
And reeled but were not drunk with wine.

For all night long I dreamed of you:
I woke and prayed against my will,
Then slept to dream of you again.
At length I rose and knelt and prayed:
I cannot write the words I said,
My words were slow, my tears were few;
But through the dark my silence spoke
Like thunder. When this morning broke,
My face was pinched, my hair was grey,

And frozen blood was on the sill
Where stifling in my struggle I lay.

If now you saw me you would say:
Where is the face I used to love?
And I would answer: Gone before;
It tarries veiled in paradise.
When once the morning star shall rise,
When earth with shadow flees away
And we stand safe within the door,
Then you shall lift the veil thereof.
Look up, rise up: for far above
Our palms are grown, our place is set;
There we shall meet as once we met
And love with old familiar love.

Up-Hill

Does the road wind up-hill all the way?
   Yes, to the very end.
Will the day's journey take the whole long day?
   From morn to night, my friend.

But is there for the night a resting-place?
   A roof for when the slow dark hours begin.
May not the darkness hide it from my face?
   You cannot miss that inn.

Shall I meet other wayfarers at night?
   Those who have gone before.
Then must I knock, or call when just in sight?
   They will not keep you standing at that door.

Shall I find comfort, travel-sore and weak?
   Of labour you shall find the sum.
Will there be beds for me and all who seek?
   Yea, beds for all who come.

"A Bruised Reed Shall He Not Break"

I will accept thy will to do and be,
   Thy hatred and intolerance of sin,
   Thy will at least to love, that burns within
      And thirsteth after Me:
So will I render fruitful, blessing still,
   The germs and small beginnings in thy heart,
   Because thy will cleaves to the better part. —
      Alas, I cannot will.

Dost not thou will, poor soul? Yet I receive
   The inner unseen longings of the soul,
   I guide them turning towards Me; I control
      And charm hearts till they grieve:
If thou desire, it yet shall come to pass,
   Though thou but wish indeed to choose My love;
   For I have power in earth and heaven above. —
      I cannot wish, alas!

What, neither choose nor wish to choose? and yet
   I still must strive to win thee and constrain:
   For thee I hung upon the cross in pain,
      How then can I forget?
If thou as yet dost neither love, nor hate,
   Nor choose, nor wish, — resign thyself, be still
   Till I infuse love, hatred, longing, will. —
      I do not deprecate.

A Better Resurrection

I have no wit, no words, no tears;
   My heart within me like a stone
Is numbed too much for hopes or fears;
   Look right, look left, I dwell alone;

I lift mine eyes, but dimmed with grief
  No everlasting hills I see;
My life is in the falling leaf:
  O Jesus, quicken me.

My life is like a faded leaf,
  My harvest dwindled to a husk;
Truly my life is void and brief
  And tedious in the barren dusk;
My life is like a frozen thing,
  No bud nor greenness can I see:
Yet rise it shall — the sap of Spring;
  O Jesus, rise in me.

My life is like a broken bowl,
  A broken bowl that cannot hold
One drop of water for my soul
  Or cordial in the searching cold;
Cast in the fire the perished thing,
  Melt and remould it, till it be
A royal cup for Him my King:
  O Jesus, drink of me.

The Three Enemies

THE FLESH

"Sweet, thou art pale."
                "More pale to see,
Christ hung upon the cruel tree
And bore His Father's wrath for me."

"Sweet, thou art sad."
              "Beneath a rod
More heavy, Christ for my sake trod
The winepress of the wrath of God."

"Sweet, thou art weary."
                        "Not so Christ:
Whose mighty love of me sufficed
For Strength, Salvation, Eucharist."

"Sweet, thou art footsore."
                        "If I bleed,
His feet have bled: yea, in my need
His Heart once bled for mine indeed."

THE WORLD

"Sweet, thou art young."
                       "So He was young
Who for my sake in silence hung
Upon the Cross with Passion wrung."

"Look, thou art fair."
                     "He was more fair
Than men, Who deigned for me to wear
A visage marred beyond compare."

"And thou hast riches."
                      "Daily bread:
All else is His; Who living, dead,
For me lacked where to lay His Head."

"And life is sweet."
                    "It was not so
To Him, Whose cup did overflow
With mine unutterable woe."

THE DEVIL

"Thou drinkest deep."
                     "When Christ would sup
He drained the dregs from out my cup:
So how should I be lifted up?"

"Thou shalt win Glory."
                    "In the skies,
Lord Jesus, cover up mine eyes
Lest they should look on vanities."

"Thou shalt have Knowledge."
                        "Helpless dust!
In Thee, O Lord, I put my trust:
Answer Thou for me, Wise and Just."

"And Might." —
            "Get thee behind me. Lord,
Who hast redeemed and not abhorred
My soul, oh keep it by Thy Word."

The One Certainty

SONNET

Vanity of vanities, the Preacher saith,
   All things are vanity. The eye and ear
   Cannot be filled with what they see and hear.
Like early dew, or like the sudden breath
Of wind, or like the grass that withereth,
   Is man, tossed to and fro by hope and fear:
   So little joy hath he, so little cheer,
Till all things end in the long dust of death.
To-day is still the same as yesterday,
   To-morrow also even as one of them;
And there is nothing new under the sun:
Until the ancient race of Time be run,
   The old thorns shall grow out of the old stem,
And morning shall be cold and twilight grey.

Sweet Death

The sweetest blossoms die.
    And so it was that, going day by day
    Unto the Church to praise and pray,
And crossing the green churchyard thoughtfully,
    I saw how on the graves the flowers
    Shed their fresh leaves in showers,
And how their perfume rose up to the sky
    Before it passed away.

The youngest blossoms die.
    They die and fall and nourish the rich earth
    From which they lately had their birth;
Sweet life, but sweeter death that passeth by
    And is as though it had not been: —
    All colours turn to green;
The bright hues vanish and the odours fly,
    The grass hath lasting worth.

And youth and beauty die.
    So be it, O my God, Thou God of truth:
    Better than beauty and than youth
Are Saints and Angels, a glad company;
    And Thou, O Lord, our Rest and Ease,
    Art better far than these.
Why should we shrink from our full harvest? why
    Prefer to glean with Ruth?

The World

SONNET

By day she woos me, soft, exceeding fair:
   But all night as the moon so changeth she;
   Loathsome and foul with hideous leprosy
And subtle serpents gliding in her hair.
By day she woos me to the outer air,
   Ripe fruit, sweet flowers, and full satiety:
   But through the night, a beast she grins at me,
A very monster void of love and prayer.
By day she stands a lie: by night she stands
   In all the naked horror of the truth
With pushing horns and clawed and clutching hands.
Is this a friend indeed; that I should sell
   My soul to her, give her my life and youth,
Till my feet, cloven too, take hold on hell?

Spring Quiet

Gone were but the Winter,
   Come were but the Spring,
I would go to a covert
   Where the birds sing;

Where in the whitethorn
   Singeth a thrush,
And a robin sings
   In the holly-bush.

Full of fresh scents
   Are the budding boughs
Arching high over
   A cool green house:

Full of sweet scents,
    And whispering air
Which sayeth softly:
    "We spread no snare;

"Here dwell in safety,
    Here dwell alone,
With a clear stream
    And a mossy stone.

"Here the sun shineth
    Most shadily;
Here is heard an echo
    Of the far sea,
    Though far off it be."

A Portrait

I

She gave up beauty in her tender youth,
    Gave up all hope and joy and pleasant ways;
    She covered up her eyes lest they should gaze
On vanity, and chose the bitter truth.
Harsh towards herself, towards others full of ruth,
    Servant of servants, little known to praise,
    Long prayers and fasts trenched on her nights and days:
She schooled herself to sights and sounds uncouth
That with the poor and stricken she might make
    A home, until the least of all sufficed
Her wants; her own self learned she to forsake,
Counting all earthly gain but hurt and loss.
So with calm will she chose and bore the cross
    And hated all for love of Jesus Christ.

II

They knelt in silent anguish by her bed,
    And could not weep; but calmly there she lay.
    All pain had left her; and the sun's last ray
Shone through upon her, warming into red
The shady curtains. In her heart she said:
    "Heaven opens; I leave these and go away;
    The Bridegroom calls, — shall the Bride seek to stay?"
Then low upon her breast she bowed her head.
O lily flower, O gem of priceless worth,
    O dove with patient voice and patient eyes,
O fruitful vine amid a land of dearth,
    O maid replete with loving purities,
Thou bowedst down thy head with friends on earth
    To raise it with the saints in Paradise.

Dream-Love

Young Love lies sleeping
    In May-time of the year,
Among the lilies,
    Lapped in the tender light:
White lambs come grazing,
    White doves come building there;
And round about him
    The May-bushes are white.

Soft moss the pillow
    For oh, a softer cheek;
Broad leaves cast shadow
    Upon the heavy eyes:
There winds and waters
    Grow lulled and scarcely speak;
There twilight lingers
    The longest in the skies.

Young Love lies dreaming;
   But who shall tell the dream?
A perfect sunlight
   On rustling forest tips;
Or perfect moonlight
   Upon a rippling stream;
Or perfect silence,
   Or song of cherished lips.

Burn odours round him
   To fill the drowsy air;
Weave silent dances
   Around him to and fro;
For oh, in waking
   The sights are not so fair,
And song and silence
   Are not like these below.

Young Love lies dreaming
   Till summer days are gone, —
Dreaming and drowsing
   Away to perfect sleep:
He sees the beauty
   Sun hath not looked upon,
And tastes the fountain
   Unutterably deep.

Him perfect music
   Doth hush unto his rest,
And through the pauses
   The perfect silence calms:
Oh, poor the voices
   Of earth from east to west,
And poor earth's stillness
   Between her stately palms.

Young Love lies drowsing
   Away to poppied death;

Cool shadows deepen
   Across the sleeping face:
So fails the summer
   With warm, delicious breath;
And what hath autumn
   To give us in its place?

Draw close the curtains
   Of branched evergreen;
Change cannot touch them
   With fading fingers sere:
Here the first violets
   Perhaps will bud unseen,
And a dove, may be,
   Return to nestle here.

Twice

I took my heart in my hand
   (O my love, O my love),
I said: Let me fall or stand,
   Let me live or die,
But this once hear me speak—
   (O my love, O my love)—
Yet a woman's words are weak;
   You should speak, not I.

You took my heart in your hand
   With a friendly smile,
With a critical eye you scanned,
   Then set it down,
And said: It is still unripe,
   Better wait awhile;
Wait while the skylarks pipe,
   Till the corn grows brown.

As you set it down it broke —
   Broke, but I did not wince;
I smiled at the speech you spoke,
   At your judgment that I heard:
But I have not often smiled
   Since then, nor questioned since,
Nor cared for corn-flowers wild,
   Nor sung with the singing bird.

I take my heart in my hand,
   O my God, O my God,
My broken heart in my hand:
   Thou hast seen, judge Thou.
My hope was written on sand,
   O my God, O my God:
Now let Thy judgment stand —
   Yea, judge me now.

This contemned of a man,
   This marred one heedless day,
This heart take Thou to scan
   Both within and without:
Refine with fire its gold,
   Purge Thou its dross away —
Yea, hold it in Thy hold,
   Whence none can pluck it out.

I take my heart in my hand —
   I shall not die, but live —
Before Thy face I stand;
   I, for Thou callest such:
All that I have I bring,
   All that I am I give,
Smile Thou and I shall sing,
   But shall not question much.

One Day

I will tell you when they met:
In the limpid days of Spring;
Elder boughs were budding yet,
Oaken boughs looked wintry still,
But primrose and veined violet
In the mossful turf were set,
While meeting birds made haste to sing
And build with right good will.

I will tell you when they parted:
When plenteous Autumn sheaves were brown,
Then they parted heavy-hearted;
The full rejoicing sun looked down
As grand as in the days before;
Only they had lost a crown;
Only to them those days of yore
Could come back nevermore.

When shall they meet? I cannot tell,
Indeed, when they shall meet again,
Except some day in Paradise:
For this they wait, one waits in pain.
Beyond the sea of death love lies
For ever, yesterday, to-day;
Angels shall ask them, "Is it well?"
And they shall answer, "Yea."

A Dream

SONNET

Once in a dream (for once I dreamed of you)
    We stood together in an open field;
    Above our heads two swift-winged pigeons wheeled,
Sporting at ease and courting full in view.
When loftier still a broadening darkness flew,
    Down-swooping, and a ravenous hawk revealed;
    Too weak to fight, too fond to fly, they yield;
So farewell life and love and pleasures new.
Then as their plumes fell fluttering to the ground,
    Their snow-white plumage flecked with crimson drops,
        I wept, and thought I turned towards you to weep:
    But you were gone; while rustling hedgerow tops
Bent in a wind which bore to me a sound
        Of far-off piteous bleat of lambs and sheep.

Beauty Is Vain

While roses are so red,
    While lilies are so white,
Shall a woman exalt her face
    Because it gives delight?
She's not so sweet as a rose,
    A lily's straighter than she,
And if she were as red or white
    She'd be but one of three.

Whether she flush in love's summer
    Or in its winter grow pale,
Whether she flaunt her beauty
    Or hide it away in a veil,

Be she red or white,
   And stand she erect or bowed,
Time will win the race he runs with her
   And hide her away in a shroud.

What Would I Give?

What would I give for a heart of flesh to warm me through,
Instead of this heart of stone ice-cold whatever I do;
Hard and cold and small, of all hearts the worst of all.

What would I give for words, if only words would come;
But now in its misery my spirit has fallen dumb:
Oh, merry friends, go your way, I have never a word to say.

What would I give for tears, not smiles but scalding tears,
To wash the black mark clean, and to thaw the frost of years,
To wash the stain ingrain and to make me clean again.

The Bourne

Underneath the growing grass,
   Underneath the living flowers,
   Deeper than the sound of showers:
   There we shall not count the hours
By the shadows as they pass.

Youth and health will be but vain,
   Beauty reckoned of no worth:
   There a very little girth
   Can hold round what once the earth
Seemed too narrow to contain.

Memory

I

I nursed it in my bosom while it lived,
   I hid it in my heart when it was dead;
In joy I sat alone, even so I grieved
     Alone and nothing said.

I shut the door to face the naked truth,
   I stood alone — I faced the truth alone,
Stripped bare of self-regard or forms or ruth
     Till first and last were shown.

I took the perfect balances and weighed;
   No shaking of my hand disturbed the poise;
Weighed, found it wanting: not a word I said,
     But silent made my choice.

None know the choice I made; I make it still.
   None know the choice I made and broke my heart,
Breaking mine idol: I have braced my will
     Once, chosen for once my part.

I broke it at a blow, I laid it cold,
   Crushed in my deep heart where it used to live.
My heart dies inch by inch; the time grows old,
     Grows old in which I grieve.

II

I have a room whereinto no one enters
   Save I myself alone:
There sits a blessed memory on a throne,
There my life centres.

While winter comes and goes — oh tedious comer! —
   And while its nip-wind blows;
   While bloom the bloodless lily and warm rose
Of lavish summer.

If any should force entrance he might see there
  One buried yet not dead,
  Before whose face I no more bow my head
Or bend my knee there;

But often in my worn life's autumn weather
  I watch there with clear eyes,
  And think how it will be in Paradise
When we're together.

Shall I Forget?

Shall I forget on this side of the grave?
I promise nothing: you must wait and see
    Patient and brave.
(O my soul, watch with him and he with me.)

Shall I forget in peace of Paradise?
I promise nothing: follow, friend, and see
    Faithful and wise.
(O my soul, lead the way he walks with me.)

Vanity of Vanities

SONNET

Ah, woe is me for pleasure that is vain,
  Ah, woe is me for glory that is past:
  Pleasure that bringeth sorrow at the last,
Glory that at the last bringeth no gain!
So saith the sinking heart; and so again
  It shall say till the mighty angel-blast
  Is blown, making the sun and moon aghast
And showering down the stars like sudden rain.

And evermore men shall go fearfully
   Bending beneath their weight of heaviness;
And ancient men shall lie down wearily,
   And strong men shall rise up in weariness;
Yea, even the young shall answer sighingly
   Saying one to another: How vain it is!

L.E.L.

'Whose heart was breaking for a little love.'

Downstairs I laugh, I sport and jest with all:
   But in my solitary room above
I turn my face in silence to the wall;
   My heart is breaking for a little love.
     Though winter frosts are done,
     And birds pair every one,
And leaves peep out, for springtide is begun.

I feel no spring, while spring is wellnigh blown,
   I find no nest, while nests are in the grove:
Woe's me for mine own heart that dwells alone,
   My heart that breaketh for a little love.
     While golden in the sun
     Rivulets rise and run,
While lilies bud, for springtide is begun.

All love, are loved, save only I; their hearts
   Beat warm with love and joy, beat full thereof:
They cannot guess, who play the pleasant parts,
   My heart is breaking for a little love.
     While beehives wake and whirr,
     And rabbit thins his fur,
In living spring that sets the world astir.

I deck myself with silks and jewelry,
   I plume myself like any mated dove:

They praise my rustling show, and never see
   My heart is breaking for a little love.
     While sprouts green lavender
     With rosemary and myrrh,
For in quick spring the sap is all astir.

Perhaps some saints in glory guess the truth,
   Perhaps some angels read it as they move,
And cry one to another full of ruth,
   "Her heart is breaking for a little love."
     Though other things have birth,
     And leap and sing for mirth,
When springtime wakes and clothes and feeds the earth.

Yet saith a saint: "Take patience for thy scathe;"
   Yet saith an angel: "Wait, for thou shalt prove
True best is last, true life is born of death,
   O thou, heart-broken for a little love.
     Then love shall fill thy girth,
     And love make fat thy dearth,
When new spring builds new heaven and clean new earth."

Life and Death

Life is not sweet. One day it will be sweet
   To shut our eyes and die:
Nor feel the wild flowers blow, nor birds dart by
   With flitting butterfly,
Nor grass grow long above our heads and feet,
Nor hear the happy lark that soars sky high,
Nor sigh that spring is fleet and summer fleet,
   Nor mark the waxing wheat,
Nor know who sits in our accustomed seat.

Life is not good. One day it will be good
   To die, then live again;
To sleep meanwhile: so not to feel the wane

Of shrunk leaves dropping in the wood,
Nor hear the foamy lashing of the main,
Nor mark the blackened bean-fields, nor where stood
    Rich ranks of golden grain
Only dead refuse stubble clothe the plain:
Asleep from risk, asleep from pain.

Grown and Flown

I loved my love from green of Spring
    Until sere Autumn's fall;
But now that leaves are withering
    How should one love at all?
    One heart's too small
For hunger, cold, love, everything.

I loved my love on sunny days
    Until late Summer's wane;
But now that frost begins to glaze
    How should one love again?
    Nay, love and pain
Walk wide apart in diverse ways.

I loved my love — alas to see
    That this should be, alas!
I thought that this could scarcely be,
    Yet has it come to pass:
    Sweet sweet love was,
Now bitter bitter grown to me.

Despised and Rejected

My sun has set, I dwell
In darkness as a dead man out of sight;
And none remains, not one, that I should tell
To him mine evil plight
This bitter night.
I will make fast my door
That hollow friends may trouble me no more.

"Friend, open to Me." — Who is this that calls?
Nay, I am deaf as are my walls:
Cease crying, for I will not hear
Thy cry of hope or fear.
Others were dear,
Others forsook me: what art thou indeed
That I should heed
Thy lamentable need?
Hungry should feed,
Or stranger lodge thee here?

"Friend, My Feet bleed.
Open thy door to Me and comfort Me."
I will not open, trouble me no more.
Go on thy way footsore,
I will not rise and open unto thee.
"Then is it nothing to thee? Open, see
Who stands to plead with thee.
Open, lest I should pass thee by, and thou
One day entreat My Face
And howl for grace,
And I be deaf as thou art now.
Open to Me."

Then I cried out upon him: Cease,
Leave me in peace:
Fear not that I should crave

Aught thou mayst have.
Leave me in peace, yea trouble me no more,
Lest I arise and chase thee from my door.
What, shall I not be let
Alone, that thou dost vex me yet?

But all night long that voice spake urgently:
"Open to Me."
Still harping in mine ears:
"Rise, let Me in."
Pleading with tears:
"Open to Me that I may come to thee."
While the dew dropped, while the dark hours were cold:
"My Feet bleed, see My Face,
See My Hands bleed that bring thee grace,
My Heart doth bleed for thee,
Open to Me."

So till the break of day:
Then died away
That voice, in silence as of sorrow;
Then footsteps echoing like a sigh
Passed me by,
Lingering footsteps slow to pass.
On the morrow
I saw upon the grass
Each footprint marked in blood, and on my door
The mark of blood for evermore.

The Lowest Place

Give me the lowest place: not that I dare
    Ask for that lowest place, but Thou hast died
That I might live and share
    Thy glory by Thy side.

    Give me the lowest place: or if for me
       That lowest place too high, make one more low
    Where I may sit and see
       My God and love Thee so.

Consider

        Consider
The lilies of the field whose bloom is brief: —
       We are as they;
       Like them we fade away,
As doth a leaf.

        Consider
The sparrows of the air of small account:
       Our God doth view
Whether they fall or mount, —
       He guards us too.

        Consider
The lilies that do neither spin nor toil,
       Yet are most fair: —
       What profits all this care
And all this coil?

        Consider
The birds that have no barn nor harvest-weeks;
       God gives them food: —
Much more our Father seeks
       To do us good.

A Smile and a Sigh

A smile because the nights are short!
    And every morning brings such pleasure
Of sweet love-making, harmless sport:
    Love, that makes and finds its treasure;
    Love, treasure without measure.

A sigh because the days are long!
    Long long these days that pass in sighing,
A burden saddens every song:
    While time lags who should be flying,
    We live who would be dying.

Paradise: In a Dream

Once in a dream I saw the flowers
    That bud and bloom in Paradise;
    More fair they are than waking eyes
Have seen in all this world of ours.
And faint the perfume-bearing rose,
    And faint the lily on its stem,
And faint the perfect violet
      Compared with them.

I heard the songs of Paradise:
    Each bird sat singing in his place;
    A tender song so full of grace
It soared like incense to the skies.
Each bird sat singing to his mate
    Soft cooing notes among the trees:
The nightingale herself were cold
      To such as these.

I saw the fourfold River flow,
   And deep it was, with golden sand;
   It flowed between a mossy land
With murmured music grave and low.
It hath refreshment for all thirst,
   For fainting spirits strength and rest;
Earth holds not such a draught as this
     From east to west.

The Tree of Life stood budding there,
   Abundant with its twelvefold fruits;
   Eternal sap sustains its roots,
Its shadowing branches fill the air.
Its leaves are healing for the world,
   Its fruit the hungry world can feed,
Sweeter than honey to the taste
     And balm indeed.

I saw the gate called Beautiful;
   And looked, but scarce could look within;
   I saw the golden streets begin,
And outskirts of the glassy pool.
Oh harps, oh crowns of plenteous stars,
   Oh green palm branches many-leaved—
Eye hath not seen, nor ear hath heard,
     Nor heart conceived.

I hope to see these things again,
   But not as once in dreams by night;
   To see them with my very sight,
And touch and handle and attain:
To have all Heaven beneath my feet
   For narrow way that once they trod;
To have my part with all the saints,
     And with my God.

Sleeping at Last

Sleeping at last, the trouble and tumult over,
   Sleeping at last, the struggle and horror past,
Cold and white, out of sight of friend and of lover,
      Sleeping at last.

   No more a tired heart downcast or overcast,
No more pangs that wring or shifting fears that hover,
   Sleeping at last in a dreamless sleep locked fast.

Fast asleep. Singing birds in their leafy cover
   Cannot wake her, nor shake her the gusty blast.
Under the purple thyme and the purple clover
      Sleeping at last.

Alphabetical List of Titles

After Death	22
An Apple Gathering	25
Another Spring	30
At Home	17
Beauty Is Vain	52
Better Resurrection, A	40
Birthday, A	21
Bourne, The	53
"Bruised Reed Shall He Not Break, A"	40
Consider	61
Convent Threshold, The	35
Cousin Kate	19
Despised and Rejected	59
Dream, A	52
Dream Land	16
Dream-Love	47
Echo	28
End, An	23
First Spring Day, The	34
Goblin Market	1
Grown and Flown	58
L.E.L.	56
Life and Death	57
Lowest Place, The	60
Maude Clare	26
May	32

Memory	54
"No, Thank You, John"	30
One Certainty, The	43
One Day	51
Paradise: In a Dream	62
Pause of Thought, A	32
Portrait, A	46
Remember	22
Shall I Forget?	55
Sister Maude	33
Sleeping at Last	64
Smile and a Sigh, A	62
Song ("Oh roses for the flush of youth")	24
Song ("Two doves upon the selfsame branch")	26
Song ("When I am dead, my dearest")	33
Spring	20
Spring Quiet	45
Summer Wish, A	24
Sweet Death	44
Three Enemies, The	41
Triad, A	18
Twice	49
Up-Hill	39
Vanity of Vanities	55
What Would I Give?	53
Winter: My Secret	28
World, The	45

Alphabetical List of First Lines

Ah, woe is me for pleasure that is vain	55
A smile because the nights are short!	62
By day she woos me, soft, exceeding fair	45
Come to me in the silence of the night	28
Consider	61
Does the road wind up-hill all the way?	39
Downstairs I laugh, I sport and jest with all	56
Frost-locked all the winter	20
Give me the lowest place: not that I dare	60
Gone were but the Winter	45
I cannot tell you how it was	32
If I might see another Spring	30
I have no wit, no words, no tears	40
I looked for that which is not, nor can be	32
I loved my love from green of Spring	58
I never said I loved you, John	30
I nursed it in my bosom while it lived	54
I plucked pink blossoms from mine apple-tree	25
I tell my secret? No indeed, not I	28
I took my heart in my hand	49
I was a cottage maiden	19
I will accept thy will to do and be	40
I will tell you when they met	51
I wonder if the sap is stirring yet	34
Life is not sweet. One day it will be sweet	57
Live all thy sweet life thro'	24

Love, strong as Death, is dead	23
Morning and evening	1
My heart is like a singing bird	21
My sun has set, I dwell	59
Oh roses for the flush of youth	24
Once in a dream (for once I dreamed of you)	52
Once in a dream I saw the flowers	62
Out of the church she followed them	26
Remember me when I am gone away	22
Shall I forget on this side of the grave?	55
She gave up beauty in her tender youth	46
Sleeping at last, the trouble and tumult over	64
"Sweet, thou art pale." "More pale to see"	41
The curtains were half drawn, the floor was swept	22
There's blood between us, love, my love	35
The sweetest blossoms die	44
Three sang of love together: one with lips	18
Two doves upon the selfsame branch	26
Underneath the growing grass	53
Vanity of vanities, the Preacher saith	43
What would I give for a heart of flesh to warm me through	53
When I am dead, my dearest	33
When I was dead, my spirit turned	17
Where sunless rivers weep	16
While roses are so red	52
Who told my mother of my shame	33
Young Love lies sleeping	47

DOVER · THRIFT · EDITIONS

Selected Poems
EMILY DICKINSON

DOVER PUBLICATIONS, INC.
New York

DOVER THRIFT EDITIONS
Editor: Stanley Appelbaum

This Dover edition, first published in 1990, contains the complete text of 109 poems exactly as they were printed in the three volumes from the 1890s listed in the Note to the present edition.

Manufactured in the United States of America
Dover Publications, Inc.
31 East 2nd Street
Mineola, N.Y. 11501

Library of Congress Cataloging-in-Publication Data

Dickinson, Emily, 1830–1886.
  [Poems. Selections]
  Selected poems / Emily Dickinson.
    p.   cm. — (Dover thrift editions)
  "This Dover edition . . . contains the complete text of 109 poems exactly as they were printed in the three volumes from the 1890s listed in the note to the present edition"—T.p. verso.
  Includes index.
  ISBN 0-486-26466-1 (pbk.)
  I. Title. II. Series.
  PS1541.A6   1990
811'.4—dc20   90-37717
                                          CIP

Note

EMILY DICKINSON (1830–1886) is still considered America's foremost woman poet. Of her more than 1,700 extant poems, only a handful were published in her lifetime. She never married and she seldom left her family home in Amherst, Massachusetts, but she transcended all physical limitations in her extensive, artistic correspondence and, even more so, in her unflinchingly honest, psychologically penetrating and technically adventurous poems.

One hundred nine of her best and best-remembered works are reprinted here exactly* as they appeared in the first three posthumous anthologies: the 1890 volume (*Poems by Emily Dickinson / Edited by two of her friends / Mabel Loomis Todd and T. W. Higginson,* Roberts Brothers, Boston [the 16th edition, 1897, was the specific source]), the 1891 volume (same title as above, plus *Second Series* [the 5th edition, 1893, was the specific source]) and the 1896 volume (same title as for 1890, plus *Third Series* [1st edition was source]). The titles (such as "Escape" and "Compensation") given to some of the poems by the early editors are retained here for completeness, but since they were not original with the poet, they have not been entered in any table of contents or index of titles. An index of first lines has been provided, however, at the end of this volume.

The best and handiest source of dates of original composition (usually only approximate) is *The Complete Poems of Emily Dickinson,* edited by Thomas H. Johnson, Little, Brown and Company, Boston, n.d. (ca. 1960; a simplified edition of that editor's complete variorum edition of 1955). The following dates of the 109 selections in the Dover edition are based on Johnson's research.

Ca. 1858: "It's all I have to bring to-day" (Dover page 1).

Ca. 1859: "I never hear the word 'escape' " (page 1) through "For each ecstatic instant" (page 2).

Ca. 1860: "The thought beneath so slight a film" and "I taste a liquor never brewed" (both page 2), as well as "I'll tell you how the sun rose" (page 11).

v

1861 (or ca. 1861): "Safe in their alabaster chambers" (page 3) through "It's like the light,—" (page 10), as well as "The nearest dream recedes, unrealized" (page 12).

1862 (or ca. 1862): "A long, long sleep, a famous sleep" (page 10) through "Of all the souls that stand create" (page 32), with the exception of "I'll tell you how the sun rose" (page 11), "The nearest dream recedes, unrealized" (page 12) and "I years had been from home" (page 28).

Ca. 1863: "One need not be a chamber to be haunted" (page 32) through "Her final summer was it" (page 39).

Ca. 1864: "A light exists in spring" (page 39) through "A door just opened on a street—" (page 43).

Ca. 1865: "A narrow fellow in the grass" (page 44) through "I never saw a moor" (page 45).

Ca. 1866: "The sky is low, the clouds are mean" (page 45) through "The cricket sang" (page 46).

Ca. 1869: "After a hundred years" (page 46).

Ca. 1871: "Before you thought of spring" (page 47).

Ca. 1872: "I years had been from home" (page 28) and "The show is not the show" (page 47).

Ca. 1873: "There is no frigate like a book" and "So proud she was to die" (both page 48).

1878: "We like March, his shoes are purple" (page 48).

Ca. 1884: "The pedigree of honey" (page 49).

Undated: "My life closed twice before its close" (page 49).

---

*Except that the almost certainly correct reading "cleaving" has been substituted for the original edition's "clearing" in the first line of "I felt a cleaving in my mind" (page 43).

Contents

The Poems   1

Index of First Lines   51

It's all I have to bring to-day,
    This, and my heart beside,
This, and my heart, and all the fields,
    And all the meadows wide.
Be sure you count, should I forget,—
    Some one the sum could tell,—
This, and my heart, and all the bees
    Which in the clover dwell.

Escape.

I never hear the word "escape"
Without a quicker blood,
A sudden expectation,
A flying attitude.

I never hear of prisons broad
By soldiers battered down,
But I tug childish at my bars,—
Only to fail again!

So bashful when I spied her,
So pretty, so ashamed!
So hidden in her leaflets,
Lest anybody find;

So breathless till I passed her,
So helpless when I turned
And bore her, struggling, blushing,
Her simple haunts beyond!

For whom I robbed the dingle,
For whom betrayed the dell,
Many will doubtless ask me,
But I shall never tell!

My nosegays are for captives;
    Dim, long-expectant eyes,
Fingers denied the plucking,
    Patient till paradise.

To such, if they should whisper
    Of morning and the moor,
They bear no other errand,
    And I, no other prayer.

Compensation.

For each ecstatic instant
We must an anguish pay
In keen and quivering ratio
To the ecstasy.

For each beloved hour
Sharp pittances of years,
Bitter contested farthings
And coffers heaped with tears.

The thought beneath so slight a film
Is more distinctly seen,—
As laces just reveal the surge,
Or mists the Apennine.

I taste a liquor never brewed,
From tankards scooped in pearl;
Not all the vats upon the Rhine
Yield such an alcohol!

Inebriate of air am I,
And debauchee of dew,
Reeling, through endless summer days,
From inns of molten blue.

When landlords turn the drunken bee
Out of the foxglove's door,
When butterflies renounce their drams,
I shall but drink the more!

Till seraphs swing their snowy hats,
And saints to windows run,
To see the little tippler
Leaning against the sun!

Safe in their alabaster chambers,
Untouched by morning and untouched by noon,
Sleep the meek members of the resurrection,
Rafter of satin, and roof of stone.

Light laughs the breeze in her castle of sunshine;
Babbles the bee in a stolid ear;
Pipe the sweet birds in ignorant cadence,—
Ah, what sagacity perished here!

Grand go the years in the crescent above them;
Worlds scoop their arcs, and firmaments row,
Diadems drop and Doges surrender,
Soundless as dots on a disk of snow.

She sweeps with many-colored brooms,
And leaves the shreds behind;
Oh, housewife in the evening west,
Come back, and dust the pond!

You dropped a purple ravelling in,
You dropped an amber thread;
And now you've littered all the East
With duds of emerald!

And still she plies her spotted brooms,
And still the aprons fly,
Till brooms fade softly into stars —
And then I come away.

Playmates.

God permits industrious angels
Afternoons to play.
I met one, — forgot my school-mates,
All, for him, straightway.

God calls home the angels promptly
At the setting sun;
I missed mine. How dreary marbles,
After playing Crown!

Forbidden Fruit.
II.

Heaven is what I cannot reach!
  The apple on the tree,
Provided it do hopeless hang,
  That 'heaven' is, to me.

The color on the cruising cloud,
  The interdicted ground
Behind the hill, the house behind, —
  There Paradise is found!

The Lost Jewel.

I held a jewel in my fingers
And went to sleep.
The day was warm, and winds were prosy;
I said: "'T will keep."

I woke and chid my honest fingers, —
The gem was gone;
And now an amethyst remembrance
Is all I own.

Wild nights! Wild nights!
Were I with thee,
Wild nights should be
Our luxury!

Futile the winds
To a heart in port, —
Done with the compass,
Done with the chart.

Rowing in Eden!
Ah! the sea!
Might I but moor
To-night in thee!

Hope.

Hope is the thing with feathers
That perches in the soul,
And sings the tune without the words,
And never stops at all,

And sweetest in the gale is heard;
And sore must be the storm
That could abash the little bird
That kept so many warm.

I've heard it in the chillest land,
And on the strangest sea;
Yet, never, in extremity,
It asked a crumb of me.

There's a certain slant of light,
On winter afternoons,
That oppresses, like the weight
Of cathedral tunes.

Heavenly hurt it gives us;
We can find no scar,
But internal difference
Where the meanings are.

None may teach it anything,
'T is the seal, despair,—
An imperial affliction
Sent us of the air.

When it comes, the landscape listens,
Shadows hold their breath;
When it goes, 't is like the distance
On the look of death.

&

Good night! which put the candle out?
A jealous zephyr, not a doubt.
   Ah! friend, you little knew
How long at that celestial wick
The angels labored diligent;
   Extinguished, now, for you!

It might have been the lighthouse spark
Some sailor, rowing in the dark,
   Had importuned to see!
It might have been the waning lamp
That lit the drummer from the camp
   To purer reveille!

The Sea of Sunset.

This is the land the sunset washes,
These are the banks of the Yellow Sea;
Where it rose, or whither it rushes,
These are the western mystery!

Night after night her purple traffic
Strews the landing with opal bales;

Merchantmen poise upon horizons,
Dip, and vanish with fairy sails.

❧

I breathed enough to learn the trick,
    And now, removed from air,
I simulate the breath so well,
    That one, to be quite sure

The lungs are stirless, must descend
    Among the cunning cells,
And touch the pantomime himself.
    How cool the bellows feels!

❧

The only ghost I ever saw
Was dressed in mechlin,—so;
He wore no sandal on his foot,
And stepped like flakes of snow.
His gait was soundless, like the bird,
But rapid, like the roe;
His fashions quaint, mosaic,
Or, haply, mistletoe.

His conversation seldom,
His laughter like the breeze
That dies away in dimples
Among the pensive trees.
Our interview was transient,—
Of me, himself was shy;
And God forbid I look behind
Since that appalling day!

❧

A shady friend for torrid days
Is easier to find

Than one of higher temperature
For frigid hour of mind.

The vane a little to the east
Scares muslin souls away;
If broadcloth breasts are firmer
Than those of organdy,

Who is to blame? The weaver?
Ah! the bewildering thread!
The tapestries of paradise
So notelessly are made!

Farewell.

Tie the strings to my life, my Lord,
    Then I am ready to go!
Just a look at the horses—
    Rapid! That will do!

Put me in on the firmest side,
    So I shall never fall;
For we must ride to the Judgment,
    And it's partly down hill.

But never I mind the bridges,
    And never I mind the sea;
Held fast in everlasting race
    By my own choice and thee.

Good-by to the life I used to live,
    And the world I used to know;
And kiss the hills for me, just once;
    Now I am ready to go!

I felt a funeral in my brain,
    And mourners, to and fro,
Kept treading, treading, till it seemed
    That sense was breaking through.

And when they all were seated,
  A service like a drum
Kept beating, beating, till I thought
  My mind was going numb.

And then I heard them lift a box,
  And creak across my soul
With those same boots of lead, again.
  Then space began to toll

As all the heavens were a bell,
  And Being but an ear,
And I and silence some strange race,
  Wrecked, solitary, here.

Clock.

A clock stopped—not the mantel's;
  Geneva's farthest skill
Can't put the puppet bowing
  That just now dangled still.

An awe came on the trinket!
  The figures hunched with pain,
Then quivered out of decimals
  Into degreeless noon.

It will not stir for doctors,
  This pendulum of snow;
The shopman importunes it,
  While cool, concernless No

Nods from the gilded pointers,
  Nods from the seconds slim,
Decades of arrogance between
  The dial life and him.

I'm nobody! Who are you?
Are you nobody, too?

Then there's a pair of us—don't tell!
They'd banish us, you know.

How dreary to be somebody!
How public, like a frog
To tell your name the livelong day
To an admiring bog!

The Wind.

It's like the light,—
    A fashionless delight
It's like the bee,—
    A dateless melody.

It's like the woods,
    Private like breeze,
Phraseless, yet it stirs
    The proudest trees.

It's like the morning,—
    Best when it's done,—
The everlasting clocks
    Chime noon.

Sleeping.

A long, long sleep, a famous sleep
That makes no show for dawn
By stretch of limb or stir of lid,—
An independent one.

Was ever idleness like this?
Within a hut of stone
To bask the centuries away
Nor once look up for noon?

Day's Parlor.

The day came slow, till five o'clock,
Then sprang before the hills

Like hindered rubies, or the light
A sudden musket spills.

The purple could not keep the east,
The sunrise shook from fold,
Like breadths of topaz, packed a night,
The lady just unrolled.

The happy winds their timbrels took;
The birds, in docile rows,
Arranged themselves around their prince
(The wind is prince of those).

The orchard sparkled like a Jew, —
How mighty 't was, to stay
A guest in this stupendous place,
The parlor of the day!

The Master.

He fumbles at your spirit
    As players at the keys
Before they drop full music on;
    He stuns you by degrees,

Prepares your brittle substance
    For the ethereal blow,
By fainter hammers, further heard,
    Then nearer, then so slow

Your breath has time to straighten,
    Your brain to bubble cool, —
Deals one imperial thunderbolt
    That scalps your naked soul.

A Day.

I'll tell you how the sun rose, —
A ribbon at a time.
The steeples swam in amethyst,
The news like squirrels ran.

The hills untied their bonnets,
The bobolinks begun.
Then I said softly to myself,
"That must have been the sun!"
. . . .
But how he set, I know not.
There seemed a purple stile
Which little yellow boys and girls
Were climbing all the while

Till when they reached the other side,
A dominie in gray
Put gently up the evening bars,—
And led the flock away.

ଈ

The nearest dream recedes, unrealized.
    The heaven we chase
    Like the June bee
    Before the school-boy
    Invites the race;
    Stoops to an easy clover—
Dips—evades—teases—deploys;
    Then to the royal clouds
    Lifts his light pinnace
    Heedless of the boy
Staring, bewildered, at the mocking sky.

    Homesick for steadfast honey,
    Ah! the bee flies not
That brews that rare variety.

ଈ

We play at paste,
Till qualified for pearl,
Then drop the paste,
And deem ourself a fool.
The shapes, though, were similar,
And our new hands

Learned gem-tactics
Practising sands.

In the Garden.

A bird came down the walk:
He did not know I saw;
He bit an angle-worm in halves
And ate the fellow, raw.

And then he drank a dew
From a convenient grass,
And then hopped sidewise to the wall
To let a beetle pass.

He glanced with rapid eyes
That hurried all abroad,—
They looked like frightened beads, I thought;
He stirred his velvet head

Like one in danger; cautious,
I offered him a crumb,
And he unrolled his feathers
And rowed him softer home

Than oars divide the ocean,
Too silver for a seam,
Or butterflies, off banks of noon,
Leap, plashless, as they swim.

I know a place where summer strives
With such a practised frost,
She each year leads her daisies back,
Recording briefly, "Lost."

But when the south wind stirs the pools
And struggles in the lanes,
Her heart misgives her for her vow,
And she pours soft refrains

Into the lap of adamant,
And spices, and the dew,

That stiffens quietly to quartz,
Upon her amber shoe.

In Shadow.

I dreaded that first robin so,
But he is mastered now,
And I'm accustomed to him grown,—
He hurts a little, though.

I thought if I could only live
Till that first shout got by,
Not all pianos in the woods
Had power to mangle me.

I dared not meet the daffodils,
For fear their yellow gown
Would pierce me with a fashion
So foreign to my own.

I wished the grass would hurry,
So when 't was time to see,
He'd be too tall, the tallest one
Could stretch to look at me.

I could not bear the bees should come,
I wished they'd stay away
In those dim countries where they go:
What word had they for me?

They're here, though; not a creature failed,
No blossom stayed away
In gentle deference to me,
The Queen of Calvary.

Each one salutes me as he goes,
And I my childish plumes
Lift, in bereaved acknowledgment
Of their unthinking drums.

Memorials.

Death sets a thing significant
The eye had hurried by,
Except a perished creature
Entreat us tenderly

To ponder little workmanships
In crayon or in wool,
With "This was last her fingers did,"
Industrious until

The thimble weighed too heavy,
The stitches stopped themselves,
And then 't was put among the dust
Upon the closet shelves.

A book I have, a friend gave,
Whose pencil, here and there,
Had notched the place that pleased him,—
At rest his fingers are.

Now, when I read, I read not,
For interrupting tears
Obliterate the etchings
Too costly for repairs.

The Soul's Storm.

It struck me every day
　　The lightning was as new
As if the cloud that instant slit
　　And let the fire through.

It burned me in the night,
　　It blistered in my dream;
It sickened fresh upon my sight
　　With every morning's beam.

I thought that storm was brief,—
    The maddest, quickest by;
But Nature lost the date of this,
    And left it in the sky.

※

I went to heaven,—
'T was a small town,
Lit with a ruby,
Lathed with down.
Stiller than the fields
At the full dew,
Beautiful as pictures
No man drew.
People like the moth,
Of mechlin, frames,
Duties of gossamer,
And eider names.
Almost contented
I could be
'Mong such unique
Society.

※

There's been a death in the opposite house
    As lately as to-day.
I know it by the numb look
    Such houses have alway.

The neighbors rustle in and out,
    The doctor drives away.
A window opens like a pod,
    Abrupt, mechanically;

Somebody flings a mattress out,—
    The children hurry by;
They wonder if It died on that,—
    I used to when a boy.

The minister goes stiffly in
    As if the house were his,
And he owned all the mourners now,
    And little boys besides;

And then the milliner, and the man
    Of the appalling trade,
To take the measure of the house.
    There'll be that dark parade

Of tassels and of coaches soon;
    It's easy as a sign,—
The intuition of the news
    In just a country town.

The Battlefield.

They dropped like flakes, they dropped like stars,
    Like petals from a rose,
When suddenly across the June
    A wind with fingers goes.

They perished in the seamless grass,—
    No eye could find the place;
But God on his repealless list
    Can summon every face.

The First Lesson.

Not in this world to see his face
Sounds long, until I read the place
Where this is said to be
But just the primer to a life
Unopened, rare, upon the shelf,
Clasped yet to him and me.

And yet, my primer suits me so
I would not choose a book to know
Than that, be sweeter wise;

Might some one else so learned be,
And leave me just my A B C,
Himself could have the skies.

Me! Come! My dazzled face
In such a shining place!

Me! Hear! My foreign ear
The sounds of welcome near!

The saints shall meet
Our bashful feet.

My holiday shall be
That they remember me;

My paradise, the fame
That they pronounce my name.

The Wind's Visit.

The wind tapped like a tired man,
And like a host, "Come in,"
I boldly answered; entered then
My residence within

A rapid, footless guest,
To offer whom a chair
Were as impossible as hand
A sofa to the air.

No bone had he to bind him,
His speech was like the push
Of numerous humming-birds at once
From a superior bush.

His countenance a billow,
His fingers, if he pass,
Let go a music, as of tunes
Blown tremulous in glass.

He visited, still flitting;
Then, like a timid man,
Again he tapped—'t was flurriedly—
And I became alone.

≥●

This is my letter to the world,
    That never wrote to me,—
The simple news that Nature told,
    With tender majesty.

Her message is committed
    To hands I cannot see;
For love of her, sweet countrymen,
    Judge tenderly of me!

Fringed Gentian.

God made a little gentian;
It tried to be a rose
And failed, and all the summer laughed.
But just before the snows
There came a purple creature
That ravished all the hill;
And summer hid her forehead,
And mockery was still.
The frosts were her condition;
The Tyrian would not come
Until the North evoked it.
"Creator! shall I bloom?"

Retrospect.

'T was just this time last year I died.
    I know I heard the corn,
When I was carried by the farms,—
    It had the tassels on.

I thought how yellow it would look
  When Richard went to mill;
And then I wanted to get out,
  But something held my will.

I thought just how red apples wedged
  The stubble's joints between;
And carts went stooping round the fields
  To take the pumpkins in.

I wondered which would miss me least,
  And when Thanksgiving came,
If father'd multiply the plates
  To make an even sum.

And if my stocking hung too high,
  Would it blur the Christmas glee,
That not a Santa Claus could reach
  The altitude of me?

But this sort grieved myself, and so
  I thought how it would be
When just this time, some perfect year,
  Themselves should come to me.

&

I died for beauty, but was scarce
Adjusted in the tomb,
When one who died for truth was lain
In an adjoining room.

He questioned softly why I failed?
"For beauty," I replied.
"And I for truth,—the two are one;
We brethren are," he said.

And so, as kinsmen met a night,
We talked between the rooms,
Until the moss had reached our lips,
And covered up our names.

Dying.

I heard a fly buzz when I died;
    The stillness round my form
Was like the stillness in the air
    Between the heaves of storm.

The eyes beside had wrung them dry,
    And breaths were gathering sure
For that last onset, when the king
    Be witnessed in his power.

I willed my keepsakes, signed away
    What portion of me I
Could make assignable,—and then
    There interposed a fly,

With blue, uncertain, stumbling buzz,
    Between the light and me;
And then the windows failed, and then
    I could not see to see.

I had no time to hate, because
The grave would hinder me,
And life was not so ample I
Could finish enmity.

Nor had I time to love, but since
Some industry must be,
The little toil of love, I thought,
Was large enough for me.

The Letter.

"Going to him! Happy letter! Tell him—
Tell him the page I didn't write;
Tell him I only said the syntax,
And left the verb and the pronoun out.

Tell him just how the fingers hurried,
Then how they waded, slow, slow, slow;
And then you wished you had eyes in your pages,
So you could see what moved them so.

"Tell him it wasn't a practised writer,
You guessed, from the way the sentence toiled;
You could hear the bodice tug, behind you,
As if it held but the might of a child;
You almost pitied it, you, it worked so.
Tell him—No, you may quibble there,
For it would split his heart to know it,
And then you and I were silenter.

"Tell him night finished before we finished,
And the old clock kept neighing 'day!'
And you got sleepy and begged to be ended—
What could it hinder so, to say?
Tell him just how she sealed you, cautious,
But if he ask where you are hid
Until to-morrow,—happy letter!
Gesture, coquette, and shake your head!"

&

It was not death, for I stood up,
And all the dead lie down;
It was not night, for all the bells
Put out their tongues, for noon.

It was not frost, for on my flesh
I felt siroccos crawl,—
Nor fire, for just my marble feet
Could keep a chancel cool.

And yet it tasted like them all;
The figures I have seen
Set orderly, for burial,
Reminded me of mine,

As if my life were shaven
And fitted to a frame,
And could not breathe without a key;
And 't was like midnight, some,

When everything that ticked has stopped,
And space stares, all around,
Or grisly frosts, first autumn morns,
Repeal the beating ground.

But most like chaos,—stopless, cool,—
Without a chance or spar,—
Or even a report of land
To justify despair.

1862

If you were coming in the fall,
I'd brush the summer by
With half a smile and half a spurn,
As housewives do a fly.

If I could see you in a year,
I'd wind the months in balls,
And put them each in separate drawers,
Until their time befalls.

If only centuries delayed,
I'd count them on my hand,
Subtracting till my fingers dropped
Into Van Diemen's land. — Tazmania

If certain, when this life was out,
That yours and mine should be,
I'd toss it yonder like a rind,
And taste eternity. taste / take (original)

But now, all ignorant of the length
Of time's uncertain wing,
It goads me, like the goblin bee,
That will not state its sting.

Astra Castra.

Departed to the judgment,
A mighty afternoon;
Great clouds like ushers leaning,
Creation looking on.

The flesh surrendered, cancelled,
The bodiless begun;
Two worlds, like audiences, disperse,
And leave the soul alone.

Two Voyagers.

Two butterflies went out at noon
And waltzed above a stream,
Then stepped straight through the firmament
And rested on a beam;

And then together bore away
Upon a shining sea,—
Though never yet, in any port,
Their coming mentioned be.

If spoken by the distant bird,
If met in ether sea
By frigate or by merchantman,
Report was not to me.

&

The heart asks pleasure first,
And then, excuse from pain;
And then, those little anodynes
That deaden suffering;

And then, to go to sleep;
And then, if it should be

The will of its Inquisitor,
The liberty to die.

The brain within its groove
Runs evenly and true;
But let a splinter swerve,
'T were easier for you
To put the water back
When floods have slit the hills,
And scooped a turnpike for themselves,
And blotted out the mills!

Griefs.

I measure every grief I meet
   With analytic eyes;
I wonder if it weighs like mine,
   Or has an easier size.

I wonder if they bore it long,
   Or did it just begin?
I could not tell the date of mine,
   It feels so old a pain.

I wonder if it hurts to live,
   And if they have to try,
And whether, could they choose between,
   They would not rather die.

I wonder if when years have piled—
   Some thousands—on the cause
Of early hurt, if such a lapse
   Could give them any pause;

Or would they go on aching still
   Through centuries above,
Enlightened to a larger pain
   By contrast with the love.

The grieved are many, I am told;
   The reason deeper lies,—
Death is but one and comes but once,
   And only nails the eyes.

There's grief of want, and grief of cold,—
   A sort they call 'despair;'
There's banishment from native eyes,
   In sight of native air.

And though I may not guess the kind
   Correctly, yet to me
A piercing comfort it affords
   In passing Calvary,

To note the fashions of the cross,
   Of those that stand alone,
Still fascinated to presume
   That some are like my own.

Delight becomes pictorial
When viewed through pain,—
More fair, because impossible
That any gain.

The mountain at a given distance
In amber lies;
Approached, the amber flits a little,—
And that's the skies!

Hunger.

I had been hungry all the years;
My noon had come, to dine;
I, trembling, drew the table near,
And touched the curious wine.

'T was this on tables I had seen,
When turning, hungry, lone,

I looked in windows, for the wealth
I could not hope to own.

I did not know the ample bread,
'T was so unlike the crumb
The birds and I had often shared
In Nature's dining-room.

The plenty hurt me, 't was so new,—
Myself felt ill and odd,
As berry of a mountain bush
Transplanted to the road.

Nor was I hungry; so I found
That hunger was a way
Of persons outside windows,
The entering takes away.

I found the phrase to every thought
I ever had, but one;
And that defies me,—as a hand
Did try to chalk the sun

To races nurtured in the dark;—
How would your own begin?
Can blaze be done in cochineal,
Or noon in mazarin?

The Railway Train.

I like to see it lap the miles,
And lick the valleys up,
And stop to feed itself at tanks;
And then, prodigious, step

Around a pile of mountains,
And, supercilious, peer
In shanties by the sides of roads;
And then a quarry pare

To fit its sides, and crawl between,
Complaining all the while
In horrid, hooting stanza;
Then chase itself down hill

And neigh like Boanerges;
Then, punctual as a star,
Stop—docile and omnipotent—
At its own stable door.

Returning.

I years had been from home,
And now, before the door,
I dared not open, lest a face
I never saw before

Stare vacant into mine
And ask my business there.
My business,—just a life I left,
Was such still dwelling there?

I fumbled at my nerve,
I scanned the windows near;
The silence like an ocean rolled,
And broke against my ear.

I laughed a wooden laugh
That I could fear a door,
Who danger and the dead had faced,
But never quaked before.

I fitted to the latch
My hand, with trembling care,
Lest back the awful door should spring,
And leave me standing there.

I moved my fingers off
As cautiously as glass,
And held my ears, and like a thief
Fled gasping from the house.

The Journey.

Our journey had advanced;
Our feet were almost come
To that odd fork in Being's road,
Eternity by term.

Our pace took sudden awe,
Our feet reluctant led.
Before were cities, but between,
The forest of the dead.

Retreat was out of hope, —
Behind, a sealed route,
Eternity's white flag before,
And God at every gate.

In Vain.

I cannot live with you,
It would be life,
And life is over there
Behind the shelf

The sexton keeps the key to,
Putting up
Our life, his porcelain,
Like a cup

Discarded of the housewife,
Quaint or broken;
A newer Sèvres pleases,
Old ones crack.

I could not die with you,
For one must wait
To shut the other's gaze down, —
You could not.

And I, could I stand by
And see you freeze,
Without my right of frost,
Death's privilege?

Nor could I rise with you,
Because your face
Would put out Jesus',
That new grace

Glow plain and foreign
On my homesick eye,
Except that you, than he
Shone closer by.

They'd judge us—how?
For you served Heaven, you know,
Or sought to;
I could not,

Because you saturated sight,
And I had no more eyes
For sordid excellence
As Paradise.

And were you lost, I would be,
Though my name
Rang loudest
On the heavenly fame.

And were you saved,
And I condemned to be
Where you were not,
That self were hell to me.

So we must keep apart,
You there, I here,
With just the door ajar
That oceans are,
And prayer,
And that pale sustenance,
Despair!

Bequest.

You left me, sweet, two legacies,—
A legacy of love
A Heavenly Father would content,
Had He the offer of;

You left me boundaries of pain
Capacious as the sea,
Between eternity and time,
Your consciousness and me.

 ̀ ̀

A little road not made of man,
Enabled of the eye,
Accessible to thill of bee,
Or cart of butterfly.

If town it have, beyond itself,
'T is that I cannot say;
I only sigh,—no vehicle
Bears me along that way.

The Mystery of Pain.

Pain has an element of blank;
It cannot recollect
When it began, or if there were
A day when it was not.

It has no future but itself,
Its infinite realms contain
Its past, enlightened to perceive
New periods of pain.

Choice.

Of all the souls that stand create
I have elected one.
When sense from spirit files away,
And subterfuge is done;

When that which is and that which was
Apart, intrinsic, stand,
And this brief tragedy of flesh
Is shifted like a sand;

When figures show their royal front
And mists are carved away,—
Behold the atom I preferred
To all the lists of clay!

Ghosts.

One need not be a chamber to be haunted,
One need not be a house;
The brain has corridors surpassing
Material place.

Far safer, of a midnight meeting
External ghost,
Than an interior confronting
That whiter host.

Far safer through an Abbey gallop,
The stones achase,
Than, moonless, one's own self encounter
In lonesome place.

Ourself, behind ourself concealed,
Should startle most;
Assassin, hid in our apartment,
Be horror's least.

The prudent carries a revolver,
He bolts the door,
O'erlooking a superior spectre
More near.

The Goal.

Each life converges to some centre
Expressed or still;
Exists in every human nature
A goal,

Admitted scarcely to itself, it may be,
Too fair
For credibility's temerity
To dare.

Adored with caution, as a brittle heaven,
To reach
Were hopeless as the rainbow's raiment
To touch,

Yet persevered toward, surer for the distance;
How high
Unto the saints' slow diligence
The sky!

Ungained, it may be, by a life's low venture,
But then,
Eternity enables the endeavoring
Again.

They say that 'time assuages,'—
   Time never did assuage;
An actual suffering strengthens,
   As sinews do, with age.

Time is a test of trouble,
   But not a remedy.
If such it prove, it prove too
   There was no malady.

Victory comes late,
And is held low to freezing lips
Too rapt with frost
To take it.
How sweet it would have tasted,
Just a drop!
Was God so economical?
His table's spread too high for us
Unless we dine on tip-toe.
Crumbs fit such little mouths,
Cherries suit robins;
The eagle's golden breakfast
Strangles them.
God keeps his oath to sparrows,
Who of little love
Know how to starve!

A thought went up my mind to-day
That I have had before,
But did not finish,—some way back,
I could not fix the year,

Nor where it went, nor why it came
The second time to me,
Nor definitely what it was,
Have I the art to say.

But somewhere in my soul, I know
I've met the thing before;
It just reminded me—'t was all—
And came my way no more.

The Chariot.

Because I could not stop for Death,
He kindly stopped for me;
The carriage held but just ourselves
And Immortality.

We slowly drove, he knew no haste,
And I had put away
My labor, and my leisure too,
For his civility.

We passed the school where children played,
Their lessons scarcely done;
We passed the fields of gazing grain,
We passed the setting sun.

We paused before a house that seemed
A swelling of the ground;
The roof was scarcely visible,
The cornice but a mound.

Since then 't is centuries; but each
Feels shorter than the day
I first surmised the horses' heads
Were toward eternity.

&

I meant to find her when I came;
   Death had the same design;
But the success was his, it seems,
   And the discomfit mine.

I meant to tell her how I longed
   For just this single time;
But Death had told her so the first,
   And she had hearkened him.

To wander now is my abode;
   To rest,—to rest would be
A privilege of hurricane
   To memory and me.

The Wife.

She rose to his requirement, dropped
The playthings of her life
To take the honorable work
Of woman and of wife.

If aught she missed in her new day
Of amplitude, or awe,
Or first prospective, or the gold
In using wore away,

It lay unmentioned, as the sea
Develops pearl and weed,
But only to himself is known
The fathoms they abide.

Disenchantment.

It dropped so low in my regard
    I heard it hit the ground,
And go to pieces on the stones
    At bottom of my mind;

Yet blamed the fate that fractured, less
    Than I reviled myself
For entertaining plated wares
    Upon my silver shelf.

Presentiment is that long shadow on the lawn
Indicative that suns go down;
The notice to the startled grass
That darkness is about to pass.

I lived on dread; to those who know
The stimulus there is
In danger, other impetus
Is numb and vital-less.

As 't were a spur upon the soul,
A fear will urge it where
To go without the spectre's aid
Were challenging despair.

Mother Nature.

Nature, the gentlest mother,
Impatient of no child,
The feeblest or the waywardest,
Her admonition mild

In forest and the hill
By traveller is heard,
Restraining rampant squirrel
Or too impetuous bird.

How fair her conversation,
A summer afternoon,—
Her household, her assembly;
And when the sun goes down

Her voice among the aisles
Incites the timid prayer
Of the minutest cricket,
The most unworthy flower.

When all the children sleep
She turns as long away
As will suffice to light her lamps;
Then, bending from the sky

With infinite affection
And infiniter care,

Her golden finger on her lip,
Wills silence everywhere.

Enough.

God gave a loaf to every bird,
But just a crumb to me;
I dare not eat it, though I starve,—
My poignant luxury
To own it, touch it, prove the feat
That made the pellet mine,—
Too happy in my sparrow chance
For ampler coveting.

It might be famine all around,
I could not miss an ear,
Such plenty smiles upon my board,
My garner shows so fair.
I wonder how the rich may feel,—
An Indiaman—an Earl?
I deem that I with but a crumb
Am sovereign of them all.

Summer Shower.

A drop fell on the apple tree,
Another on the roof;
A half a dozen kissed the eaves,
And made the gables laugh.

A few went out to help the brook,
That went to help the sea.
Myself conjectured, Were they pearls,
What necklaces could be!

The dust replaced in hoisted roads,
The birds jocoser sung;
The sunshine threw his hat away,
The orchards spangles hung.

The breezes brought dejected lutes,
And bathed them in the glee;

The East put out a single flag,
And signed the fête away.

At Length.

Her final summer was it,
And yet we guessed it not;
If tenderer industriousness
Pervaded her, we thought

A further force of life
Developed from within,—
When Death lit all the shortness up,
And made the hurry plain.

We wondered at our blindness,—
When nothing was to see
But her Carrara guide-post,—
At our stupidity,

When, duller than our dulness,
The busy darling lay,
So busy was she, finishing,
So leisurely were we!

ॐ

A light exists in spring
   Not present on the year
At any other period.
   When March is scarcely here

A color stands abroad
   On solitary hills
That science cannot overtake,
   But human nature *feels*.

It waits upon the lawn;
   It shows the furthest tree
Upon the furthest slope we know;
   It almost speaks to me.

Then, as horizons step,
   Or noons report away,

Without the formula of sound,
    It passes, and we stay:

A quality of loss
    Affecting our content,
As trade had suddenly encroached
    Upon a sacrament.

A Thunder-storm.

The wind begun to rock the grass
With threatening tunes and low, —
He flung a menace at the earth,
A menace at the sky.

The leaves unhooked themselves from trees
And started all abroad;
The dust did scoop itself like hands
And throw away the road.

The wagons quickened on the streets,
The thunder hurried slow;
The lightning showed a yellow beak,
And then a livid claw.

The birds put up the bars to nests,
The cattle fled to barns;
There came one drop of giant rain,
And then, as if the hands

That held the dams had parted hold,
The waters wrecked the sky,
But overlooked my father's house,
Just quartering a tree.

A Country Burial.

Ample make this bed.
Make this bed with awe;
In it wait till judgment break
Excellent and fair.

Be its mattress straight,
Be its pillow round;
Let no sunrise' yellow noise
Interrupt this ground.

Experience.

I stepped from plank to plank
    So slow and cautiously;
The stars about my head I felt,
    About my feet the sea.

I knew not but the next
    Would be my final inch,—
This gave me that precarious gait
    Some call experience.

The Sea.

An everywhere of silver,
With ropes of sand
To keep it from effacing
The track called land.

We outgrow love like other things
    And put it in the drawer,
Till it an antique fashion shows
    Like costumes grandsires wore.

To my quick ear the leaves conferred;
    The bushes they were bells;

I could not find a privacy
    From Nature's sentinels.

In cave if I presumed to hide,
    The walls began to tell;
Creation seemed a mighty crack
    To make me visible.

The Bee.

Like trains of cars on tracks of plush
I hear the level bee:
A jar across the flowers goes,
Their velvet masonry

Withstands until the sweet assault
Their chivalry consumes,
While he, victorious, tilts away
To vanquish other blooms.

His feet are shod with gauze,
His helmet is of gold;
His breast, a single onyx
With chrysoprase, inlaid.

His labor is a chant,
His idleness a tune;
Oh, for a bee's experience
Of clovers and of noon!

If I can stop one heart from breaking,
I shall not live in vain;
If I can ease one life the aching,
Or cool one pain,
Or help one fainting robin
Unto his nest again,
I shall not live in vain.

The Lost Thought.

I felt a cleaving in my mind
    As if my brain had split;
I tried to match it, seam by seam,
    But could not make them fit.

The thought behind I strove to join
    Unto the thought before,
But sequence ravelled out of reach
    Like balls upon a floor.

Immortality.

It is an honorable thought,
    And makes one lift one's hat,
As one encountered gentlefolk
    Upon a daily street,

That we've immortal place,
    Though pyramids decay,
And kingdoms, like the orchard,
    Flit russetly away.

Contrast.

A door just opened on a street—
    I, lost, was passing by—
An instant's width of warmth disclosed,
    And wealth, and company.

The door as sudden shut, and I,
    I, lost, was passing by,—
Lost doubly, but by contrast most,
    Enlightening misery.

The Snake.

A narrow fellow in the grass
Occasionally rides;
You may have met him,—did you not,
His notice sudden is.

The grass divides as with a comb,
A spotted shaft is seen;
And then it closes at your feet
And opens further on.

He likes a boggy acre,
A floor too cool for corn.
Yet when a child, and barefoot,
I more than once, at morn,

Have passed, I thought, a whip-lash
Unbraiding in the sun,—
When, stooping to secure it,
It wrinkled, and was gone.

Several of nature's people
I know, and they know me;
I feel for them a transport
Of cordiality;

But never met this fellow,
Attended or alone,
Without a tighter breathing,
And zero at the bone.

The dying need but little, dear,—
   A glass of water's all,
A flower's unobtrusive face
   To punctuate the wall,

A fan, perhaps, a friend's regret,
   And certainly that one

No color in the rainbow
    Perceives when you are gone.

Nature rarer uses yellow
Than another hue;
Saves she all of that for sunsets,—
Prodigal of blue,

Spending scarlet like a woman,
Yellow she affords
Only scantly and selectly,
Like a lover's words.

I never saw a moor,
I never saw the sea;
Yet know I how the heather looks,
And what a wave must be.

I never spoke with God,
Nor visited in heaven;
Yet certain am I of the spot
As if the chart were given.

Beclouded.

The sky is low, the clouds are mean,
A travelling flake of snow
Across a barn or through a rut
Debates if it will go.

A narrow wind complains all day
How some one treated him;

Nature, like us, is sometimes caught
Without her diadem.

The bustle in a house
The morning after death
Is solemnest of industries
Enacted upon earth, —

The sweeping up the heart,
And putting love away
We shall not want to use again
Until eternity.

Evening.

The cricket sang,
And set the sun,
And workmen finished, one by one,
　　Their seam the day upon.

The low grass loaded with the dew,
The twilight stood as strangers do
With hat in hand, polite and new,
　　To stay as if, or go.

A vastness, as a neighbor, came, —
A wisdom without face or name,
A peace, as hemispheres at home, —
　　And so the night became.

The Forgotten Grave.

After a hundred years
Nobody knows the place, —
Agony, that enacted there,
Motionless as peace.

Weeds triumphant ranged,
Strangers strolled and spelled
At the lone orthography
Of the elder dead.

Winds of summer fields
Recollect the way,—
Instinct picking up the key
Dropped by memory.

The Bluebird.

Before you thought of spring,
Except as a surmise,
You see, God bless his suddenness,
A fellow in the skies
Of independent hues,
A little weather-worn,
Inspiriting habiliments
Of indigo and brown.

With specimens of song,
As if for you to choose,
Discretion in the interval,
With gay delays he goes
To some superior tree
Without a single leaf,
And shouts for joy to nobody
But his seraphic self!

The Show.

The show is not the show,
But they that go.
Menagerie to me
My neighbor be.
Fair play—
Both went to see.

A Book.

There is no frigate like a book
    To take us lands away,
Nor any coursers like a page
    Of prancing poetry.
This traverse may the poorest take
    Without oppress of toll;
How frugal is the chariot
    That bears a human soul!

So proud she was to die
    It made us all ashamed
That what we cherished, so unknown
    To her desire seemed.

So satisfied to go
    Where none of us should be,
Immediately, that anguish stooped
    Almost to jealousy.

March.

We like March, his shoes are purple,
    He is new and high;
Makes he mud for dog and peddler,
    Makes he forest dry;
Knows the adder's tongue his coming,
    And begets her spot.
Stands the sun so close and mighty
    That our minds are hot.
News is he of all the others;
    Bold it were to die
With the blue-birds buccaneering
    On his British sky.

The pedigree of honey
Does not concern the bee;
A clover, any time, to him
Is aristocracy.

Parting.

My life closed twice before its close;
    It yet remains to see
If Immortality unveil
    A third event to me,

So huge, so hopeless to conceive,
    As these that twice befell.
Parting is all we know of heaven,
    And all we need of hell.

Index of First Lines

page

A bird came down the walk	13
A clock stopped—not the mantel's	9
A door just opened on a street—	43
A drop fell on the apple tree	38
After a hundred years	46
A light exists in spring	39
A little road not made of man	31
A long, long sleep, a famous sleep	10
Ample make this bed	40
A narrow fellow in the grass	44
An everywhere of silver	41
A shady friend for torrid days	7
A thought went up my mind to-day	34
Because I could not stop for Death	35
Before you thought of spring	47
Death sets a thing significant	15
Delight becomes pictorial	26
Departed to the judgment	24
Each life converges to some centre	33
For each ecstatic instant	2
God gave a loaf to every bird	38
God made a little gentian	19
God permits industrious angels	4
"Going to him! Happy letter! Tell him—"	21

	page
Good night! which put the candle out?	6
Heaven is what I cannot reach!	4
He fumbles at your spirit	11
Her final summer was it	39
Hope is the thing with feathers	5
I breathed enough to learn the trick	7
I cannot live with you	29
I died for beauty, but was scarce	20
I dreaded that first robin so	14
I felt a cleaving in my mind	43
I felt a funeral in my brain	8
If I can stop one heart from breaking	42
I found the phrase to every thought	27
If you were coming in the fall	23
I had been hungry all the years	26
I had no time to hate, because	21
I heard a fly buzz when I died	21
I held a jewel in my fingers	4
I know a place where summer strives	13
I like to see it lap the miles	27
I lived on dread: to those who know	37
I'll tell you how the sun rose,—	11
I meant to find her when I came	35
I measure every grief I meet	25
I'm nobody! Who are you?	9
I never hear the word "escape"	1
I never saw a moor	45
I stepped from plank to plank	41
I taste a liquor never brewed	2
It dropped so low in my regard	36

	page
It is an honorable thought	43
It's all I have to bring to-day	1
It's like the light,—	10
It struck me every day	15
It was not death, for I stood up	22
I went to heaven,—	16
I years had been from home	28
Like trains of cars on tracks of plush	42
Me! Come! My dazzled face	18
My life closed twice before its close	49
My nosegays are for captives	2
Nature rarer uses yellow	45
Nature, the gentlest mother	37
Not in this world to see his face	17
Of all the souls that stand create	32
One need not be a chamber to be haunted	32
Our journey had advanced	29
Pain has an element of blank	31
Presentiment is that long shadow on the lawn	36
Safe in their alabaster chambers	3
She rose to his requirement, dropped	36
She sweeps with many-colored brooms	3
So bashful when I spied her	1
So proud she was to die	48
The brain within its groove	25
The bustle in a house	46
The cricket sang	46
The day came so slow, till five o'clock	10
The dying need but little, dear,—	44
The heart asks pleasure first	24

page

The nearest dream recedes, unrealized	12
The only ghost I ever saw	7
The pedigree of honey	49
There is no frigate like a book	48
There's a certain slant of light	5
There's been a death in the opposite house	16
The show is not the show	47
The sky is low, the clouds are mean	45
The thought beneath so slight a film	2
The wind begun to rock the grass	40
The wind tapped like a tired man	18
They dropped like flakes, they dropped like stars	17
They say that 'time assuages'—	33
This is my letter to the world	19
This is the land the sunset washes	6
Tie the strings to my life, my Lord	8
To my quick ear the leaves conferred	41
'T was just this time last year I died	19
Two butterflies went out at noon	24
Victory comes late	34
We like March, his shoes are purple	48
We outgrow love like other things	41
We play at paste	12
Wild nights! Wild nights!	5
You left me, sweet, two legacies,—	31

DOVER · THRIFT · EDITIONS

All books complete and unabridged. All 5³⁄₁₆″ × 8¼″, paperbound.
Just $1.00–$2.00 in U.S.A.

A selection of the more than 100 titles in the series:

FLATLAND: A ROMANCE OF MANY DIMENSIONS, Edwin A. Abbott. 96pp. 27263-X $1.00

DOVER BEACH AND OTHER POEMS, Matthew Arnold. 112pp. 28037-3 $1.00

CIVIL WAR STORIES, Ambrose Bierce. 128pp. 28038-1 $1.00

THE DEVIL'S DICTIONARY, Ambrose Bierce. 144pp. 27542-6 $1.00

SONGS OF INNOCENCE AND SONGS OF EXPERIENCE, William Blake. 64pp. 27051-3 $1.00

SONNETS FROM THE PORTUGUESE AND OTHER POEMS, Elizabeth Barrett Browning. 64pp. 27052-1 $1.00

MY LAST DUCHESS AND OTHER POEMS, Robert Browning. 128pp. 27783-6 $1.00

SELECTED POEMS, George Gordon, Lord Byron. 112pp. 27784-4 $1.00

ALICE'S ADVENTURES IN WONDERLAND, Lewis Carroll. 96pp. 27543-4 $1.00

O PIONEERS!, Willa Cather. 128pp. 27785-2 $1.00

THE CHERRY ORCHARD, Anton Chekhov. 64pp. 26682-6 $1.00

THE AWAKENING, Kate Chopin. 128pp. 27786-0 $1.00

THE RIME OF THE ANCIENT MARINER AND OTHER POEMS, Samuel Taylor Coleridge. 80pp. 27266-4 $1.00

HEART OF DARKNESS, Joseph Conrad. 80pp. 26464-5 $1.00

THE RED BADGE OF COURAGE, Stephen Crane. 112pp. 26465-3 $1.00

A CHRISTMAS CAROL, Charles Dickens. 80pp. 26865-9 $1.00

THE CRICKET ON THE HEARTH AND OTHER CHRISTMAS STORIES, Charles Dickens. 128pp. 28039-X $1.00

SELECTED POEMS, Emily Dickinson. 64pp. 26466-1 $1.00

SELECTED POEMS, John Donne. 96pp. 27788-7 $1.00

NOTES FROM THE UNDERGROUND, Fyodor Dostoyevsky. 96pp. 27053-X $1.00

SIX GREAT SHERLOCK HOLMES STORIES, Sir Arthur Conan Doyle. 112pp. 27055-6 $1.00

THE SOULS OF BLACK FOLK, W. E. B. Du Bois. 176pp. 28041-1 $2.00

MEDEA, Euripides. 64pp. 27548-5 $1.00

A BOY'S WILL AND NORTH OF BOSTON, Robert Frost. 112pp. (Available in U.S. only) 26866-7 $1.00

WHERE ANGELS FEAR TO TREAD, E. M. Forster. 128pp. (Available in U.S. only) 27791-7 $1.00

FAUST, PART ONE, Johann Wolfgang von Goethe. 192pp. 28046-2 $2.00

THE SCARLET LETTER, Nathaniel Hawthorne. 192pp. 28048-9 $2.00

A DOLL'S HOUSE, Henrik Ibsen. 80pp. 27062-9 $1.00

THE TURN OF THE SCREW, Henry James. 96pp. 26684-2 $1.00

VOLPONE, Ben Jonson. 112pp. 28049-7 $1.00

DUBLINERS, James Joyce. 160pp. 26870-5 $1.00

A PORTRAIT OF THE ARTIST AS A YOUNG MAN, James Joyce. 192pp. 28050-0 $2.00

LYRIC POEMS, John Keats. 80pp. 26871-3 $1.00

THE BOOK OF PSALMS, King James Bible. 144pp. 27541-8 $1.00

DOVER · THRIFT · EDITIONS

Selected Poems
EMILY DICKINSON

DOVER PUBLICATIONS, INC.
New York

DOVER THRIFT EDITIONS
Editor: Stanley Appelbaum

Published in Canada by General Publishing Company, Ltd.,
30 Lesmill Road, Don Mills, Toronto, Ontario.
Published in the United Kingdom by Constable and Company, Ltd.

This Dover edition, first published in 1990, contains the complete text of 109 poems exactly as they were printed in the three volumes from the 1890s listed in the Note to the present edition.

Manufactured in the United States of America
Dover Publications, Inc.
31 East 2nd Street
Mineola, N.Y. 11501

Library of Congress Cataloging-in-Publication Data

Dickinson, Emily, 1830–1886.
[Poems. Selections]
Selected poems / Emily Dickinson.
p. cm. — (Dover thrift editions)
"This Dover edition . . . contains the complete text of 109 poems exactly as they were printed in the three volumes from the 1890s listed in the note to the present edition"—T.p. verso.
Includes index.
ISBN 0-486-26466-1 (pbk.)
I. Title. II. Series.
PS1541.A6 1990
811'.4—dc20   90-37717
                              CIP

Note

EMILY DICKINSON (1830–1886) is still considered America's foremost woman poet. Of her more than 1,700 extant poems, only a handful were published in her lifetime. She never married and she seldom left her family home in Amherst, Massachusetts, but she transcended all physical limitations in her extensive, artistic correspondence and, even more so, in her unflinchingly honest, psychologically penetrating and technically adventurous poems.

One hundred nine of her best and best-remembered works are reprinted here exactly* as they appeared in the first three posthumous anthologies: the 1890 volume (*Poems by Emily Dickinson / Edited by two of her friends / Mabel Loomis Todd and T. W. Higginson*, Roberts Brothers, Boston [the 16th edition, 1897, was the specific source]), the 1891 volume (same title as above, plus *Second Series* [the 5th edition, 1893, was the specific source]) and the 1896 volume (same title as for 1890, plus *Third Series* [1st edition was source]). The titles (such as "Escape" and "Compensation") given to some of the poems by the early editors are retained here for completeness, but since they were not original with the poet, they have not been entered in any table of contents or index of titles. An index of first lines has been provided, however, at the end of this volume.

The best and handiest source of dates of original composition (usually only approximate) is *The Complete Poems of Emily Dickinson*, edited by Thomas H. Johnson, Little, Brown and Company, Boston, n.d. (ca. 1960; a simplified edition of that editor's complete variorum edition of 1955). The following dates of the 109 selections in the Dover edition are based on Johnson's research.

Ca. 1858: "It's all I have to bring to-day" (Dover page 1).

Ca. 1859: "I never hear the word 'escape' " (page 1) through "For each ecstatic instant" (page 2).

Ca. 1860: "The thought beneath so slight a film" and "I taste a liquor never brewed" (both page 2), as well as "I'll tell you how the sun rose" (page 11).

v

1861 (or ca. 1861): "Safe in their alabaster chambers" (page 3) through "It's like the light,—" (page 10), as well as "The nearest dream recedes, unrealized" (page 12).

1862 (or ca. 1862): "A long, long sleep, a famous sleep" (page 10) through "Of all the souls that stand create" (page 32), with the exception of "I'll tell you how the sun rose" (page 11), "The nearest dream recedes, unrealized" (page 12) and "I years had been from home" (page 28).

Ca. 1863: "One need not be a chamber to be haunted" (page 32) through "Her final summer was it" (page 39).

Ca. 1864: "A light exists in spring" (page 39) through "A door just opened on a street—" (page 43).

Ca. 1865: "A narrow fellow in the grass" (page 44) through "I never saw a moor" (page 45).

Ca. 1866: "The sky is low, the clouds are mean" (page 45) through "The cricket sang" (page 46).

Ca. 1869: "After a hundred years" (page 46).

Ca. 1871: "Before you thought of spring" (page 47).

Ca. 1872: "I years had been from home" (page 28) and "The show is not the show" (page 47).

Ca. 1873: "There is no frigate like a book" and "So proud she was to die" (both page 48).

1878: "We like March, his shoes are purple" (page 48).

Ca. 1884: "The pedigree of honey" (page 49).

Undated: "My life closed twice before its close" (page 49).

---

*Except that the almost certainly correct reading "cleaving" has been substituted for the original edition's "clearing" in the first line of "I felt a cleaving in my mind" (page 43).

Contents

The Poems   1

Index of First Lines   51

It's all I have to bring to-day,
    This, and my heart beside,
This, and my heart, and all the fields,
    And all the meadows wide.
Be sure you count, should I forget,—
    Some one the sum could tell,—
This, and my heart, and all the bees
    Which in the clover dwell.

Escape.

I never hear the word "escape"
Without a quicker blood,
A sudden expectation,
A flying attitude.

I never hear of prisons broad
By soldiers battered down,
But I tug childish at my bars,—
Only to fail again!

❧

So bashful when I spied her,
So pretty, so ashamed!
So hidden in her leaflets,
Lest anybody find;

So breathless till I passed her,
So helpless when I turned
And bore her, struggling, blushing,
Her simple haunts beyond!

For whom I robbed the dingle,
For whom betrayed the dell,
Many will doubtless ask me,
But I shall never tell!

My nosegays are for captives;
    Dim, long-expectant eyes,
Fingers denied the plucking,
    Patient till paradise.

To such, if they should whisper
    Of morning and the moor,
They bear no other errand,
    And I, no other prayer.

Compensation.

For each ecstatic instant
We must an anguish pay
In keen and quivering ratio
To the ecstasy.

For each beloved hour
Sharp pittances of years,
Bitter contested farthings
And coffers heaped with tears.

The thought beneath so slight a film
Is more distinctly seen,—
As laces just reveal the surge,
Or mists the Apennine.

I taste a liquor never brewed,
From tankards scooped in pearl;
Not all the vats upon the Rhine
Yield such an alcohol!

Inebriate of air am I,
And debauchee of dew,
Reeling, through endless summer days,
From inns of molten blue.

When landlords turn the drunken bee
Out of the foxglove's door,
When butterflies renounce their drams,
I shall but drink the more!

Till seraphs swing their snowy hats,
And saints to windows run,
To see the little tippler
Leaning against the sun!

Safe in their alabaster chambers,
Untouched by morning and untouched by noon,
Sleep the meek members of the resurrection,
Rafter of satin, and roof of stone.

Light laughs the breeze in her castle of sunshine;
Babbles the bee in a stolid ear;
Pipe the sweet birds in ignorant cadence, —
Ah, what sagacity perished here!

Grand go the years in the crescent above them;
Worlds scoop their arcs, and firmaments row,
Diadems drop and Doges surrender,
Soundless as dots on a disk of snow.

She sweeps with many-colored brooms,
And leaves the shreds behind;
Oh, housewife in the evening west,
Come back, and dust the pond!

You dropped a purple ravelling in,
You dropped an amber thread;
And now you've littered all the East
With duds of emerald!

And still she plies her spotted brooms,
And still the aprons fly,
Till brooms fade softly into stars—
And then I come away.

Playmates.

God permits industrious angels
Afternoons to play.
I met one,—forgot my school-mates,
All, for him, straightway.

God calls home the angels promptly
At the setting sun;
I missed mine. How dreary marbles,
After playing Crown!

Forbidden Fruit.
II.

Heaven is what I cannot reach!
　The apple on the tree,
Provided it do hopeless hang,
　That 'heaven' is, to me.

The color on the cruising cloud,
　The interdicted ground
Behind the hill, the house behind,—
　There Paradise is found!

The Lost Jewel.

I held a jewel in my fingers
And went to sleep.
The day was warm, and winds were prosy;
I said: " 'T will keep."

I woke and chid my honest fingers,—
The gem was gone;
And now an amethyst remembrance
Is all I own.

Wild nights! Wild nights!
Were I with thee,
Wild nights should be
Our luxury!

Futile the winds
To a heart in port,—
Done with the compass,
Done with the chart.

Rowing in Eden!
Ah! the sea!
Might I but moor
To-night in thee!

Hope.

Hope is the thing with feathers
That perches in the soul,
And sings the tune without the words,
And never stops at all,

And sweetest in the gale is heard;
And sore must be the storm
That could abash the little bird
That kept so many warm.

I've heard it in the chillest land,
And on the strangest sea;
Yet, never, in extremity,
It asked a crumb of me.

There's a certain slant of light,
On winter afternoons,
That oppresses, like the weight
Of cathedral tunes.

Heavenly hurt it gives us;
We can find no scar,
But internal difference
Where the meanings are.

None may teach it anything,
'T is the seal, despair, —
An imperial affliction
Sent us of the air.

When it comes, the landscape listens,
Shadows hold their breath;
When it goes, 't is like the distance
On the look of death.

Good night! which put the candle out?
A jealous zephyr, not a doubt.
  Ah! friend, you little knew
How long at that celestial wick
The angels labored diligent;
  Extinguished, now, for you!

It might have been the lighthouse spark
Some sailor, rowing in the dark,
  Had importuned to see!
It might have been the waning lamp
That lit the drummer from the camp
  To purer reveille!

The Sea of Sunset.

This is the land the sunset washes,
These are the banks of the Yellow Sea;
Where it rose, or whither it rushes,
These are the western mystery!

Night after night her purple traffic
Strews the landing with opal bales;

Merchantmen poise upon horizons,
Dip, and vanish with fairy sails.

&

I breathed enough to learn the trick,
  And now, removed from air,
I simulate the breath so well,
  That one, to be quite sure

The lungs are stirless, must descend
  Among the cunning cells,
And touch the pantomime himself.
  How cool the bellows feels!

&

The only ghost I ever saw
Was dressed in mechlin,—so;
He wore no sandal on his foot,
And stepped like flakes of snow.
His gait was soundless, like the bird,
But rapid, like the roe;
His fashions quaint, mosaic,
Or, haply, mistletoe.

His conversation seldom,
His laughter like the breeze
That dies away in dimples
Among the pensive trees.
Our interview was transient,—
Of me, himself was shy;
And God forbid I look behind
Since that appalling day!

&

A shady friend for torrid days
Is easier to find

Than one of higher temperature
For frigid hour of mind.

The vane a little to the east
Scares muslin souls away;
If broadcloth breasts are firmer
Than those of organdy,

Who is to blame? The weaver?
Ah! the bewildering thread!
The tapestries of paradise
So notelessly are made!

Farewell.

Tie the strings to my life, my Lord,
   Then I am ready to go!
Just a look at the horses—
   Rapid! That will do!

Put me in on the firmest side,
   So I shall never fall;
For we must ride to the Judgment,
   And it's partly down hill.

But never I mind the bridges,
   And never I mind the sea;
Held fast in everlasting race
   By my own choice and thee.

Good-by to the life I used to live,
   And the world I used to know;
And kiss the hills for me, just once;
   Now I am ready to go!

I felt a funeral in my brain,
   And mourners, to and fro,
Kept treading, treading, till it seemed
   That sense was breaking through.

And when they all were seated,
    A service like a drum
Kept beating, beating, till I thought
    My mind was going numb.

And then I heard them lift a box,
    And creak across my soul
With those same boots of lead, again.
    Then space began to toll

As all the heavens were a bell,
    And Being but an ear,
And I and silence some strange race,
    Wrecked, solitary, here.

Clock.

A clock stopped—not the mantel's;
    Geneva's farthest skill
Can't put the puppet bowing
    That just now dangled still.

An awe came on the trinket!
    The figures hunched with pain,
Then quivered out of decimals
    Into degreeless noon.

It will not stir for doctors,
    This pendulum of snow;
The shopman importunes it,
    While cool, concernless No

Nods from the gilded pointers,
    Nods from the seconds slim,
Decades of arrogance between
    The dial life and him.

I'm nobody! Who are you?
Are you nobody, too?

Then there's a pair of us—don't tell!
They'd banish us, you know.

How dreary to be somebody!
How public, like a frog
To tell your name the livelong day
To an admiring bog!

The Wind.

It's like the light,—
 A fashionless delight
It's like the bee,—
 A dateless melody.

It's like the woods,
 Private like breeze,
Phraseless, yet it stirs
 The proudest trees.

It's like the morning,—
 Best when it's done,—
The everlasting clocks
 Chime noon.

Sleeping.

A long, long sleep, a famous sleep
That makes no show for dawn
By stretch of limb or stir of lid,—
An independent one.

Was ever idleness like this?
Within a hut of stone
To bask the centuries away
Nor once look up for noon?

Day's Parlor.

The day came slow, till five o'clock,
Then sprang before the hills

Like hindered rubies, or the light
A sudden musket spills.

The purple could not keep the east,
The sunrise shook from fold,
Like breadths of topaz, packed a night,
The lady just unrolled.

The happy winds their timbrels took;
The birds, in docile rows,
Arranged themselves around their prince
(The wind is prince of those).

The orchard sparkled like a Jew,—
How mighty 't was, to stay
A guest in this stupendous place,
The parlor of the day!

The Master.

He fumbles at your spirit
   As players at the keys
Before they drop full music on;
   He stuns you by degrees,

Prepares your brittle substance
   For the ethereal blow,
By fainter hammers, further heard,
   Then nearer, then so slow

Your breath has time to straighten,
   Your brain to bubble cool,—
Deals one imperial thunderbolt
   That scalps your naked soul.

A Day.

I'll tell you how the sun rose,—
A ribbon at a time.
The steeples swam in amethyst,
The news like squirrels ran.

The hills untied their bonnets,
The bobolinks begun.
Then I said softly to myself,
"That must have been the sun!"
. . . .
But how he set, I know not.
There seemed a purple stile
Which little yellow boys and girls
Were climbing all the while

Till when they reached the other side,
A dominie in gray
Put gently up the evening bars,—
And led the flock away.

The nearest dream recedes, unrealized.
  The heaven we chase
  Like the June bee
  Before the school-boy
  Invites the race;
  Stoops to an easy clover—
Dips—evades—teases—deploys;
  Then to the royal clouds
  Lifts his light pinnace
  Heedless of the boy
Staring, bewildered, at the mocking sky.

  Homesick for steadfast honey,
   Ah! the bee flies not
That brews that rare variety.

We play at paste,
Till qualified for pearl,
Then drop the paste,
And deem ourself a fool.
The shapes, though, were similar,
And our new hands

Learned gem-tactics
Practising sands.

In the Garden.

A bird came down the walk:
He did not know I saw;
He bit an angle-worm in halves
And ate the fellow, raw.

And then he drank a dew
From a convenient grass,
And then hopped sidewise to the wall
To let a beetle pass.

He glanced with rapid eyes
That hurried all abroad,—
They looked like frightened beads, I thought;
He stirred his velvet head

Like one in danger; cautious,
I offered him a crumb,
And he unrolled his feathers
And rowed him softer home

Than oars divide the ocean,
Too silver for a seam,
Or butterflies, off banks of noon,
Leap, plashless, as they swim.

I know a place where summer strives
With such a practised frost,
She each year leads her daisies back,
Recording briefly, "Lost."

But when the south wind stirs the pools
And struggles in the lanes,
Her heart misgives her for her vow,
And she pours soft refrains

Into the lap of adamant,
And spices, and the dew,

That stiffens quietly to quartz,
Upon her amber shoe.

In Shadow.

I dreaded that first robin so,
But he is mastered now,
And I'm accustomed to him grown,—
He hurts a little, though.

I thought if I could only live
Till that first shout got by,
Not all pianos in the woods
Had power to mangle me.

I dared not meet the daffodils,
For fear their yellow gown
Would pierce me with a fashion
So foreign to my own.

I wished the grass would hurry,
So when 't was time to see,
He'd be too tall, the tallest one
Could stretch to look at me.

I could not bear the bees should come,
I wished they'd stay away
In those dim countries where they go:
What word had they for me?

They're here, though; not a creature failed,
No blossom stayed away
In gentle deference to me,
The Queen of Calvary.

Each one salutes me as he goes,
And I my childish plumes
Lift, in bereaved acknowledgment
Of their unthinking drums.

Memorials.

Death sets a thing significant
The eye had hurried by,
Except a perished creature
Entreat us tenderly

To ponder little workmanships
In crayon or in wool,
With "This was last her fingers did,"
Industrious until

The thimble weighed too heavy,
The stitches stopped themselves,
And then 't was put among the dust
Upon the closet shelves.

A book I have, a friend gave,
Whose pencil, here and there,
Had notched the place that pleased him, —
At rest his fingers are.

Now, when I read, I read not,
For interrupting tears
Obliterate the etchings
Too costly for repairs.

The Soul's Storm.

It struck me every day
   The lightning was as new
As if the cloud that instant slit
   And let the fire through.

It burned me in the night,
   It blistered in my dream;
It sickened fresh upon my sight
   With every morning's beam.

I thought that storm was brief,—
    The maddest, quickest by;
But Nature lost the date of this,
    And left it in the sky.

I went to heaven,—
'T was a small town,
Lit with a ruby,
Lathed with down.
Stiller than the fields
At the full dew,
Beautiful as pictures
No man drew.
People like the moth,
Of mechlin, frames,
Duties of gossamer,
And eider names.
Almost contented
I could be
'Mong such unique
Society.

There's been a death in the opposite house
    As lately as to-day.
I know it by the numb look
    Such houses have alway.

The neighbors rustle in and out,
    The doctor drives away.
A window opens like a pod,
    Abrupt, mechanically;

Somebody flings a mattress out,—
    The children hurry by;
They wonder if It died on that,—
    I used to when a boy.

The minister goes stiffly in
   As if the house were his,
And he owned all the mourners now,
   And little boys besides;

And then the milliner, and the man
   Of the appalling trade,
To take the measure of the house.
   There'll be that dark parade

Of tassels and of coaches soon;
   It's easy as a sign,—
The intuition of the news
   In just a country town.

The Battlefield.

They dropped like flakes, they dropped like stars,
   Like petals from a rose,
When suddenly across the June
   A wind with fingers goes.

They perished in the seamless grass,—
   No eye could find the place;
But God on his repealless list
   Can summon every face.

The First Lesson.

Not in this world to see his face
Sounds long, until I read the place
Where this is said to be
But just the primer to a life
Unopened, rare, upon the shelf,
Clasped yet to him and me.

And yet, my primer suits me so
I would not choose a book to know
Than that, be sweeter wise;

Might some one else so learned be,
And leave me just my A B C,
Himself could have the skies.

Me! Come! My dazzled face
In such a shining place!

Me! Hear! My foreign ear
The sounds of welcome near!

The saints shall meet
Our bashful feet.

My holiday shall be
That they remember me;

My paradise, the fame
That they pronounce my name.

The Wind's Visit.

The wind tapped like a tired man,
And like a host, "Come in,"
I boldly answered; entered then
My residence within

A rapid, footless guest,
To offer whom a chair
Were as impossible as hand
A sofa to the air.

No bone had he to bind him,
His speech was like the push
Of numerous humming-birds at once
From a superior bush.

His countenance a billow,
His fingers, if he pass,
Let go a music, as of tunes
Blown tremulous in glass.

He visited, still flitting;
Then, like a timid man,
Again he tapped—'t was flurriedly—
And I became alone.

❧

This is my letter to the world,
   That never wrote to me,—
The simple news that Nature told,
   With tender majesty.

Her message is committed
   To hands I cannot see;
For love of her, sweet countrymen,
   Judge tenderly of me!

Fringed Gentian.

God made a little gentian;
It tried to be a rose
And failed, and all the summer laughed.
But just before the snows
There came a purple creature
That ravished all the hill;
And summer hid her forehead,
And mockery was still.
The frosts were her condition;
The Tyrian would not come
Until the North evoked it.
"Creator! shall I bloom?"

Retrospect.

'T was just this time last year I died.
   I know I heard the corn,
When I was carried by the farms,—
   It had the tassels on.

I thought how yellow it would look
    When Richard went to mill;
And then I wanted to get out,
    But something held my will.

I thought just how red apples wedged
    The stubble's joints between;
And carts went stooping round the fields
    To take the pumpkins in.

I wondered which would miss me least,
    And when Thanksgiving came,
If father'd multiply the plates
    To make an even sum.

And if my stocking hung too high,
    Would it blur the Christmas glee,
That not a Santa Claus could reach
    The altitude of me?

But this sort grieved myself, and so
    I thought how it would be
When just this time, some perfect year,
    Themselves should come to me.

ಶ

I died for beauty, but was scarce
Adjusted in the tomb,
When one who died for truth was lain
In an adjoining room.

He questioned softly why I failed?
"For beauty," I replied.
"And I for truth,—the two are one;
We brethren are," he said.

And so, as kinsmen met a night,
We talked between the rooms,
Until the moss had reached our lips,
And covered up our names.

Dying.

I heard a fly buzz when I died;
    The stillness round my form
Was like the stillness in the air
    Between the heaves of storm.

The eyes beside had wrung them dry,
    And breaths were gathering sure
For that last onset, when the king
    Be witnessed in his power.

I willed my keepsakes, signed away
    What portion of me I
Could make assignable,—and then
    There interposed a fly,

With blue, uncertain, stumbling buzz,
    Between the light and me;
And then the windows failed, and then
    I could not see to see.

I had no time to hate, because
The grave would hinder me,
And life was not so ample I
Could finish enmity.

Nor had I time to love, but since
Some industry must be,
The little toil of love, I thought,
Was large enough for me.

The Letter.

"Going to him! Happy letter! Tell him—
Tell him the page I didn't write;
Tell him I only said the syntax,
And left the verb and the pronoun out.

Tell him just how the fingers hurried,
Then how they waded, slow, slow, slow;
And then you wished you had eyes in your pages,
So you could see what moved them so.

"Tell him it wasn't a practised writer,
You guessed, from the way the sentence toiled;
You could hear the bodice tug, behind you,
As if it held but the might of a child;
You almost pitied it, you, it worked so.
Tell him—No, you may quibble there,
For it would split his heart to know it,
And then you and I were silenter.

"Tell him night finished before we finished,
And the old clock kept neighing 'day!'
And you got sleepy and begged to be ended—
What could it hinder so, to say?
Tell him just how she sealed you, cautious,
But if he ask where you are hid
Until to-morrow,—happy letter!
Gesture, coquette, and shake your head!"

It was not death, for I stood up,
And all the dead lie down;
It was not night, for all the bells
Put out their tongues, for noon.

It was not frost, for on my flesh
I felt siroccos crawl,—
Nor fire, for just my marble feet
Could keep a chancel cool.

And yet it tasted like them all;
The figures I have seen
Set orderly, for burial,
Reminded me of mine,

As if my life were shaven
And fitted to a frame,
And could not breathe without a key;
And 't was like midnight, some,

When everything that ticked has stopped,
And space stares, all around,
Or grisly frosts, first autumn morns,
Repeal the beating ground.

But most like chaos,—stopless, cool,—
Without a chance or spar,—
Or even a report of land
To justify despair.

If you were coming in the fall,
I'd brush the summer by
With half a smile and half a spurn,
As housewives do a fly.

If I could see you in a year,
I'd wind the months in balls,
And put them each in separate drawers,
Until their time befalls.

If only centuries delayed,
I'd count them on my hand,
Subtracting till my fingers dropped
Into Van Diemen's land.

If certain, when this life was out,
That yours and mine should be,
I'd toss it yonder like a rind,
And taste eternity.

But now, all ignorant of the length
Of time's uncertain wing,
It goads me, like the goblin bee,
That will not state its sting.

Astra Castra.

Departed to the judgment,
A mighty afternoon;
Great clouds like ushers leaning,
Creation looking on.

The flesh surrendered, cancelled,
The bodiless begun;
Two worlds, like audiences, disperse,
And leave the soul alone.

Two Voyagers.

Two butterflies went out at noon
And waltzed above a stream,
Then stepped straight through the firmament
And rested on a beam;

And then together bore away
Upon a shining sea,—
Though never yet, in any port,
Their coming mentioned be.

If spoken by the distant bird,
If met in ether sea
By frigate or by merchantman,
Report was not to me.

The heart asks pleasure first,
And then, excuse from pain;
And then, those little anodynes
That deaden suffering;

And then, to go to sleep;
And then, if it should be

The will of its Inquisitor,
The liberty to die.

The brain within its groove
Runs evenly and true;
But let a splinter swerve,
'T were easier for you
To put the water back
When floods have slit the hills,
And scooped a turnpike for themselves,
And blotted out the mills!

Griefs.

I measure every grief I meet
    With analytic eyes;
I wonder if it weighs like mine,
    Or has an easier size.

I wonder if they bore it long,
    Or did it just begin?
I could not tell the date of mine,
    It feels so old a pain.

I wonder if it hurts to live,
    And if they have to try,
And whether, could they choose between,
    They would not rather die.

I wonder if when years have piled—
    Some thousands—on the cause
Of early hurt, if such a lapse
    Could give them any pause;

Or would they go on aching still
    Through centuries above,
Enlightened to a larger pain
    By contrast with the love.

The grieved are many, I am told;
    The reason deeper lies,—
Death is but one and comes but once,
    And only nails the eyes.

There's grief of want, and grief of cold,—
    A sort they call 'despair;'
There's banishment from native eyes,
    In sight of native air.

And though I may not guess the kind
    Correctly, yet to me
A piercing comfort it affords
    In passing Calvary,

To note the fashions of the cross,
    Of those that stand alone,
Still fascinated to presume
    That some are like my own.

Delight becomes pictorial
When viewed through pain,—
More fair, because impossible
That any gain.

The mountain at a given distance
In amber lies;
Approached, the amber flits a little,—
And that's the skies!

Hunger.

I had been hungry all the years;
My noon had come, to dine;
I, trembling, drew the table near,
And touched the curious wine.

'T was this on tables I had seen,
When turning, hungry, lone,

I looked in windows, for the wealth
I could not hope to own.

I did not know the ample bread,
'T was so unlike the crumb
The birds and I had often shared
In Nature's dining-room.

The plenty hurt me, 't was so new,—
Myself felt ill and odd,
As berry of a mountain bush
Transplanted to the road.

Nor was I hungry; so I found
That hunger was a way
Of persons outside windows,
The entering takes away.

I found the phrase to every thought
I ever had, but one;
And that defies me,—as a hand
Did try to chalk the sun

To races nurtured in the dark;—
How would your own begin?
Can blaze be done in cochineal,
Or noon in mazarin?

The Railway Train.

I like to see it lap the miles,
And lick the valleys up,
And stop to feed itself at tanks;
And then, prodigious, step

Around a pile of mountains,
And, supercilious, peer
In shanties by the sides of roads;
And then a quarry pare

To fit its sides, and crawl between,
Complaining all the while
In horrid, hooting stanza;
Then chase itself down hill

And neigh like Boanerges;
Then, punctual as a star,
Stop—docile and omnipotent—
At its own stable door.

Returning.

I years had been from home,
And now, before the door,
I dared not open, lest a face
I never saw before

Stare vacant into mine
And ask my business there.
My business,—just a life I left,
Was such still dwelling there?

I fumbled at my nerve,
I scanned the windows near;
The silence like an ocean rolled,
And broke against my ear.

I laughed a wooden laugh
That I could fear a door,
Who danger and the dead had faced,
But never quaked before.

I fitted to the latch
My hand, with trembling care,
Lest back the awful door should spring,
And leave me standing there.

I moved my fingers off
As cautiously as glass,
And held my ears, and like a thief
Fled gasping from the house.

The Journey.

Our journey had advanced;
Our feet were almost come
To that odd fork in Being's road,
Eternity by term.

Our pace took sudden awe,
Our feet reluctant led.
Before were cities, but between,
The forest of the dead.

Retreat was out of hope,—
Behind, a sealed route,
Eternity's white flag before,
And God at every gate.

In Vain.

I cannot live with you,
It would be life,
And life is over there
Behind the shelf

The sexton keeps the key to,
Putting up
Our life, his porcelain,
Like a cup

Discarded of the housewife,
Quaint or broken;
A newer Sèvres pleases,
Old ones crack.

I could not die with you,
For one must wait
To shut the other's gaze down,—
You could not.

And I, could I stand by
And see you freeze,
Without my right of frost,
Death's privilege?

Nor could I rise with you,
Because your face
Would put out Jesus',
That new grace

Glow plain and foreign
On my homesick eye,
Except that you, than he
Shone closer by.

They'd judge us—how?
For you served Heaven, you know,
Or sought to;
I could not,

Because you saturated sight,
And I had no more eyes
For sordid excellence
As Paradise.

And were you lost, I would be,
Though my name
Rang loudest
On the heavenly fame.

And were you saved,
And I condemned to be
Where you were not,
That self were hell to me.

So we must keep apart,
You there, I here,
With just the door ajar
That oceans are,
And prayer,
And that pale sustenance,
Despair!

Bequest.

You left me, sweet, two legacies,—
A legacy of love
A Heavenly Father would content,
Had He the offer of;

You left me boundaries of pain
Capacious as the sea,
Between eternity and time,
Your consciousness and me.

A little road not made of man,
Enabled of the eye,
Accessible to thill of bee,
Or cart of butterfly.

If town it have, beyond itself,
'T is that I cannot say;
I only sigh,—no vehicle
Bears me along that way.

The Mystery of Pain.

Pain has an element of blank;
It cannot recollect
When it began, or if there were
A day when it was not.

It has no future but itself,
Its infinite realms contain
Its past, enlightened to perceive
New periods of pain.

Choice.

Of all the souls that stand create
I have elected one.
When sense from spirit files away,
And subterfuge is done;

When that which is and that which was
Apart, intrinsic, stand,
And this brief tragedy of flesh
Is shifted like a sand;

When figures show their royal front
And mists are carved away, —
Behold the atom I preferred
To all the lists of clay!

Ghosts.

One need not be a chamber to be haunted,
One need not be a house;
The brain has corridors surpassing
Material place.

Far safer, of a midnight meeting
External ghost,
Than an interior confronting
That whiter host.

Far safer through an Abbey gallop,
The stones achase,
Than, moonless, one's own self encounter
In lonesome place.

Ourself, behind ourself concealed,
Should startle most;
Assassin, hid in our apartment,
Be horror's least.

The prudent carries a revolver,
He bolts the door,
O'erlooking a superior spectre
More near.

The Goal.

Each life converges to some centre
Expressed or still;
Exists in every human nature
A goal,

Admitted scarcely to itself, it may be,
Too fair
For credibility's temerity
To dare.

Adored with caution, as a brittle heaven,
To reach
Were hopeless as the rainbow's raiment
To touch,

Yet persevered toward, surer for the distance;
How high
Unto the saints' slow diligence
The sky!

Ungained, it may be, by a life's low venture,
But then,
Eternity enables the endeavoring
Again.

They say that 'time assuages,'—
    Time never did assuage;
An actual suffering strengthens,
    As sinews do, with age.

Time is a test of trouble,
   But not a remedy.
If such it prove, it prove too
   There was no malady.

Victory comes late,
And is held low to freezing lips
Too rapt with frost
To take it.
How sweet it would have tasted,
Just a drop!
Was God so economical?
His table's spread too high for us
Unless we dine on tip-toe.
Crumbs fit such little mouths,
Cherries suit robins;
The eagle's golden breakfast
Strangles them.
God keeps his oath to sparrows,
Who of little love
Know how to starve!

A thought went up my mind to-day
That I have had before,
But did not finish,—some way back,
I could not fix the year,

Nor where it went, nor why it came
The second time to me,
Nor definitely what it was,
Have I the art to say.

But somewhere in my soul, I know
I've met the thing before;
It just reminded me—'t was all—
And came my way no more.

The Chariot.

Because I could not stop for Death,
He kindly stopped for me;
The carriage held but just ourselves
And Immortality.

We slowly drove, he knew no haste,
And I had put away
My labor, and my leisure too,
For his civility.

We passed the school where children played,
Their lessons scarcely done;
We passed the fields of gazing grain,
We passed the setting sun.

We paused before a house that seemed
A swelling of the ground;
The roof was scarcely visible,
The cornice but a mound.

Since then 't is centuries; but each
Feels shorter than the day
I first surmised the horses' heads
Were toward eternity.

I meant to find her when I came;
   Death had the same design;
But the success was his, it seems,
   And the discomfit mine.

I meant to tell her how I longed
   For just this single time;
But Death had told her so the first,
   And she had hearkened him.

To wander now is my abode;
   To rest,—to rest would be
A privilege of hurricane
   To memory and me.

The Wife.

She rose to his requirement, dropped
The playthings of her life
To take the honorable work
Of woman and of wife.

If aught she missed in her new day
Of amplitude, or awe,
Or first prospective, or the gold
In using wore away,

It lay unmentioned, as the sea
Develops pearl and weed,
But only to himself is known
The fathoms they abide.

Disenchantment.

It dropped so low in my regard
   I heard it hit the ground,
And go to pieces on the stones
   At bottom of my mind;

Yet blamed the fate that fractured, less
   Than I reviled myself
For entertaining plated wares
   Upon my silver shelf.

Presentiment is that long shadow on the lawn
Indicative that suns go down;
The notice to the startled grass
That darkness is about to pass.

🙵

I lived on dread; to those who know
The stimulus there is
In danger, other impetus
Is numb and vital-less.

As 't were a spur upon the soul,
A fear will urge it where
To go without the spectre's aid
Were challenging despair.

Mother Nature.

Nature, the gentlest mother,
Impatient of no child,
The feeblest or the waywardest,
Her admonition mild

In forest and the hill
By traveller is heard,
Restraining rampant squirrel
Or too impetuous bird.

How fair her conversation,
A summer afternoon, —
Her household, her assembly;
And when the sun goes down

Her voice among the aisles
Incites the timid prayer
Of the minutest cricket,
The most unworthy flower.

When all the children sleep
She turns as long away
As will suffice to light her lamps;
Then, bending from the sky

With infinite affection
And infiniter care,

Her golden finger on her lip,
Wills silence everywhere.

Enough.

God gave a loaf to every bird,
But just a crumb to me;
I dare not eat it, though I starve,—
My poignant luxury
To own it, touch it, prove the feat
That made the pellet mine,—
Too happy in my sparrow chance
For ampler coveting.

It might be famine all around,
I could not miss an ear,
Such plenty smiles upon my board,
My garner shows so fair.
I wonder how the rich may feel,—
An Indiaman—an Earl?
I deem that I with but a crumb
Am sovereign of them all.

Summer Shower.

A drop fell on the apple tree,
Another on the roof;
A half a dozen kissed the eaves,
And made the gables laugh.

A few went out to help the brook,
That went to help the sea.
Myself conjectured, Were they pearls,
What necklaces could be!

The dust replaced in hoisted roads,
The birds jocoser sung;
The sunshine threw his hat away,
The orchards spangles hung.

The breezes brought dejected lutes,
And bathed them in the glee;

The East put out a single flag,
And signed the fête away.

At Length.

Her final summer was it,
And yet we guessed it not;
If tenderer industriousness
Pervaded her, we thought

A further force of life
Developed from within, —
When Death lit all the shortness up,
And made the hurry plain.

We wondered at our blindness, —
When nothing was to see
But her Carrara guide-post, —
At our stupidity,

When, duller than our dulness,
The busy darling lay,
So busy was she, finishing,
So leisurely were we!

&

A light exists in spring
   Not present on the year
At any other period.
   When March is scarcely here

A color stands abroad
   On solitary hills
That science cannot overtake,
   But human nature *feels*.

It waits upon the lawn;
   It shows the furthest tree
Upon the furthest slope we know;
   It almost speaks to me.

Then, as horizons step,
   Or noons report away,

Without the formula of sound,
   It passes, and we stay:

A quality of loss
   Affecting our content,
As trade had suddenly encroached
   Upon a sacrament.

A Thunder-storm.

The wind begun to rock the grass
With threatening tunes and low,—
He flung a menace at the earth,
A menace at the sky.

The leaves unhooked themselves from trees
And started all abroad;
The dust did scoop itself like hands
And throw away the road.

The wagons quickened on the streets,
The thunder hurried slow;
The lightning showed a yellow beak,
And then a livid claw.

The birds put up the bars to nests,
The cattle fled to barns;
There came one drop of giant rain,
And then, as if the hands

That held the dams had parted hold,
The waters wrecked the sky,
But overlooked my father's house,
Just quartering a tree.

A Country Burial.

Ample make this bed.
Make this bed with awe;
In it wait till judgment break
Excellent and fair.

Be its mattress straight,
Be its pillow round;
Let no sunrise' yellow noise
Interrupt this ground.

Experience.

I stepped from plank to plank
    So slow and cautiously;
The stars about my head I felt,
    About my feet the sea.

I knew not but the next
    Would be my final inch,—
This gave me that precarious gait
    Some call experience.

The Sea.

An everywhere of silver,
With ropes of sand
To keep it from effacing
The track called land.

We outgrow love like other things
    And put it in the drawer,
Till it an antique fashion shows
    Like costumes grandsires wore.

To my quick ear the leaves conferred;
    The bushes they were bells;

I could not find a privacy
    From Nature's sentinels.

In cave if I presumed to hide,
    The walls began to tell;
Creation seemed a mighty crack
    To make me visible.

The Bee.

Like trains of cars on tracks of plush
I hear the level bee:
A jar across the flowers goes,
Their velvet masonry

Withstands until the sweet assault
Their chivalry consumes,
While he, victorious, tilts away
To vanquish other blooms.

His feet are shod with gauze,
His helmet is of gold;
His breast, a single onyx
With chrysoprase, inlaid.

His labor is a chant,
His idleness a tune;
Oh, for a bee's experience
Of clovers and of noon!

If I can stop one heart from breaking,
I shall not live in vain;
If I can ease one life the aching,
Or cool one pain,
Or help one fainting robin
Unto his nest again,
I shall not live in vain.

The Lost Thought.

I felt a cleaving in my mind
    As if my brain had split;
I tried to match it, seam by seam,
    But could not make them fit.

The thought behind I strove to join
    Unto the thought before,
But sequence ravelled out of reach
    Like balls upon a floor.

Immortality.

It is an honorable thought,
    And makes one lift one's hat,
As one encountered gentlefolk
    Upon a daily street,

That we've immortal place,
    Though pyramids decay,
And kingdoms, like the orchard,
    Flit russetly away.

Contrast.

A door just opened on a street—
    I, lost, was passing by—
An instant's width of warmth disclosed,
    And wealth, and company.

The door as sudden shut, and I,
    I, lost, was passing by,—
Lost doubly, but by contrast most,
    Enlightening misery.

The Snake.

A narrow fellow in the grass
Occasionally rides;
You may have met him,—did you not,
His notice sudden is.

The grass divides as with a comb,
A spotted shaft is seen;
And then it closes at your feet
And opens further on.

He likes a boggy acre,
A floor too cool for corn.
Yet when a child, and barefoot,
I more than once, at morn,

Have passed, I thought, a whip-lash
Unbraiding in the sun,—
When, stooping to secure it,
It wrinkled, and was gone.

Several of nature's people
I know, and they know me;
I feel for them a transport
Of cordiality;

But never met this fellow,
Attended or alone,
Without a tighter breathing,
And zero at the bone.

The dying need but little, dear,—
    A glass of water's all,
A flower's unobtrusive face
    To punctuate the wall,

A fan, perhaps, a friend's regret,
    And certainly that one

No color in the rainbow
   Perceives when you are gone.

❧

Nature rarer uses yellow
Than another hue;
Saves she all of that for sunsets,—
Prodigal of blue,

Spending scarlet like a woman,
Yellow she affords
Only scantly and selectly,
Like a lover's words.

❧

I never saw a moor,
I never saw the sea;
Yet know I how the heather looks,
And what a wave must be.

I never spoke with God,
Nor visited in heaven;
Yet certain am I of the spot
As if the chart were given.

Beclouded.

The sky is low, the clouds are mean,
A travelling flake of snow
Across a barn or through a rut
Debates if it will go.

A narrow wind complains all day
How some one treated him;

Nature, like us, is sometimes caught
Without her diadem.

ಇ

The bustle in a house
The morning after death
Is solemnest of industries
Enacted upon earth, —

The sweeping up the heart,
And putting love away
We shall not want to use again
Until eternity.

Evening.

The cricket sang,
And set the sun,
And workmen finished, one by one,
   Their seam the day upon.

The low grass loaded with the dew,
The twilight stood as strangers do
With hat in hand, polite and new,
   To stay as if, or go.

A vastness, as a neighbor, came, —
A wisdom without face or name,
A peace, as hemispheres at home, —
   And so the night became.

The Forgotten Grave.

After a hundred years
Nobody knows the place, —
Agony, that enacted there,
Motionless as peace.

Weeds triumphant ranged,
Strangers strolled and spelled
At the lone orthography
Of the elder dead.

Winds of summer fields
Recollect the way,—
Instinct picking up the key
Dropped by memory.

The Bluebird.

Before you thought of spring,
Except as a surmise,
You see, God bless his suddenness,
A fellow in the skies
Of independent hues,
A little weather-worn,
Inspiriting habiliments
Of indigo and brown.

With specimens of song,
As if for you to choose,
Discretion in the interval,
With gay delays he goes
To some superior tree
Without a single leaf,
And shouts for joy to nobody
But his seraphic self!

The Show.

The show is not the show,
But they that go.
Menagerie to me
My neighbor be.
Fair play—
Both went to see.

A Book.

There is no frigate like a book
    To take us lands away,
Nor any coursers like a page
    Of prancing poetry.
This traverse may the poorest take
    Without oppress of toll;
How frugal is the chariot
    That bears a human soul!

So proud she was to die
    It made us all ashamed
That what we cherished, so unknown
    To her desire seemed.

So satisfied to go
    Where none of us should be,
Immediately, that anguish stooped
    Almost to jealousy.

March.

We like March, his shoes are purple,
    He is new and high;
Makes he mud for dog and peddler,
    Makes he forest dry;
Knows the adder's tongue his coming,
    And begets her spot.
Stands the sun so close and mighty
    That our minds are hot.
News is he of all the others;
    Bold it were to die
With the blue-birds buccaneering
    On his British sky.

The pedigree of honey
Does not concern the bee;
A clover, any time, to him
Is aristocracy.

Parting.

My life closed twice before its close;
    It yet remains to see
If Immortality unveil
    A third event to me,

So huge, so hopeless to conceive,
    As these that twice befell.
Parting is all we know of heaven,
    And all we need of hell.

Index of First Lines

page

A bird came down the walk	13
A clock stopped—not the mantel's	9
A door just opened on a street—	43
A drop fell on the apple tree	38
After a hundred years	46
A light exists in spring	39
A little road not made of man	31
A long, long sleep, a famous sleep	10
Ample make this bed	40
A narrow fellow in the grass	44
An everywhere of silver	41
A shady friend for torrid days	7
A thought went up my mind to-day	34
Because I could not stop for Death	35
Before you thought of spring	47
Death sets a thing significant	15
Delight becomes pictorial	26
Departed to the judgment	24
Each life converges to some centre	33
For each ecstatic instant	2
God gave a loaf to every bird	38
God made a little gentian	19
God permits industrious angels	4
"Going to him! Happy letter! Tell him—"	21

page

Good night! which put the candle out?	6
Heaven is what I cannot reach!	4
He fumbles at your spirit	11
Her final summer was it	39
Hope is the thing with feathers	5
I breathed enough to learn the trick	7
I cannot live with you	29
I died for beauty, but was scarce	20
I dreaded that first robin so	14
I felt a cleaving in my mind	43
I felt a funeral in my brain	8
If I can stop one heart from breaking	42
I found the phrase to every thought	27
If you were coming in the fall	23
I had been hungry all the years	26
I had no time to hate, because	21
I heard a fly buzz when I died	21
I held a jewel in my fingers	4
I know a place where summer strives	13
I like to see it lap the miles	27
I lived on dread: to those who know	37
I'll tell you how the sun rose,—	11
I meant to find her when I came	35
I measure every grief I meet	25
I'm nobody! Who are you?	9
I never hear the word "escape"	1
I never saw a moor	45
I stepped from plank to plank	41
I taste a liquor never brewed	2
It dropped so low in my regard	36

	page
It is an honorable thought	43
It's all I have to bring to-day	1
It's like the light,—	10
It struck me every day	15
It was not death, for I stood up	22
I went to heaven,—	16
I years had been from home	28
Like trains of cars on tracks of plush	42
Me! Come! My dazzled face	18
My life closed twice before its close	49
My nosegays are for captives	2
Nature rarer uses yellow	45
Nature, the gentlest mother	37
Not in this world to see his face	17
Of all the souls that stand create	32
One need not be a chamber to be haunted	32
Our journey had advanced	29
Pain has an element of blank	31
Presentiment is that long shadow on the lawn	36
Safe in their alabaster chambers	3
She rose to his requirement, dropped	36
She sweeps with many-colored brooms	3
So bashful when I spied her	1
So proud she was to die	48
The brain within its groove	25
The bustle in a house	46
The cricket sang	46
The day came so slow, till five o'clock	10
The dying need but little, dear,—	44
The heart asks pleasure first	24

	page
The nearest dream recedes, unrealized	12
The only ghost I ever saw	7
The pedigree of honey	49
There is no frigate like a book	48
There's a certain slant of light	5
There's been a death in the opposite house	16
The show is not the show	47
The sky is low, the clouds are mean	45
The thought beneath so slight a film	2
The wind begun to rock the grass	40
The wind tapped like a tired man	18
They dropped like flakes, they dropped like stars	17
They say that 'time assuages'—	33
This is my letter to the world	19
This is the land the sunset washes	6
Tie the strings to my life, my Lord	8
To my quick ear the leaves conferred	41
'T was just this time last year I died	19
Two butterflies went out at noon	24
Victory comes late	34
We like March, his shoes are purple	48
We outgrow love like other things	41
We play at paste	12
Wild nights! Wild nights!	5
You left me, sweet, two legacies,—	31

DOVER · THRIFT · EDITIONS

All books complete and unabridged. All 5³⁄₁₆″ × 8¼″, paperbound.
Just $1.00–$2.00 in U.S.A.

A selection of the more than 100 titles in the series:

FLATLAND: A ROMANCE OF MANY DIMENSIONS, Edwin A. Abbott. 96pp. 27263-X $1.00

DOVER BEACH AND OTHER POEMS, Matthew Arnold. 112pp. 28037-3 $1.00

CIVIL WAR STORIES, Ambrose Bierce. 128pp. 28038-1 $1.00

THE DEVIL'S DICTIONARY, Ambrose Bierce. 144pp. 27542-6 $1.00

SONGS OF INNOCENCE AND SONGS OF EXPERIENCE, William Blake. 64pp. 27051-3 $1.00

SONNETS FROM THE PORTUGUESE AND OTHER POEMS, Elizabeth Barrett Browning. 64pp. 27052-1 $1.00

MY LAST DUCHESS AND OTHER POEMS, Robert Browning. 128pp. 27783-6 $1.00

SELECTED POEMS, George Gordon, Lord Byron. 112pp. 27784-4 $1.00

ALICE'S ADVENTURES IN WONDERLAND, Lewis Carroll. 96pp. 27543-4 $1.00

O PIONEERS!, Willa Cather. 128pp. 27785-2 $1.00

THE CHERRY ORCHARD, Anton Chekhov. 64pp. 26682-6 $1.00

THE AWAKENING, Kate Chopin. 128pp. 27786-0 $1.00

THE RIME OF THE ANCIENT MARINER AND OTHER POEMS, Samuel Taylor Coleridge. 80pp. 27266-4 $1.00

HEART OF DARKNESS, Joseph Conrad. 80pp. 26464-5 $1.00

THE RED BADGE OF COURAGE, Stephen Crane. 112pp. 26465-3 $1.00

A CHRISTMAS CAROL, Charles Dickens. 80pp. 26865-9 $1.00

THE CRICKET ON THE HEARTH AND OTHER CHRISTMAS STORIES, Charles Dickens. 128pp. 28039-X $1.00

SELECTED POEMS, Emily Dickinson. 64pp. 26466-1 $1.00

SELECTED POEMS, John Donne. 96pp. 27788-7 $1.00

NOTES FROM THE UNDERGROUND, Fyodor Dostoyevsky. 96pp. 27053-X $1.00

SIX GREAT SHERLOCK HOLMES STORIES, Sir Arthur Conan Doyle. 112pp. 27055-6 $1.00

THE SOULS OF BLACK FOLK, W. E. B. Du Bois. 176pp. 28041-1 $2.00

MEDEA, Euripides. 64pp. 27548-5 $1.00

A BOY'S WILL AND NORTH OF BOSTON, Robert Frost. 112pp. (Available in U.S. only) 26866-7 $1.00

WHERE ANGELS FEAR TO TREAD, E. M. Forster. 128pp. (Available in U.S. only) 27791-7 $1.00

FAUST, PART ONE, Johann Wolfgang von Goethe. 192pp. 28046-2 $2.00

THE SCARLET LETTER, Nathaniel Hawthorne. 192pp. 28048-9 $2.00

A DOLL'S HOUSE, Henrik Ibsen. 80pp. 27062-9 $1.00

THE TURN OF THE SCREW, Henry James. 96pp. 26684-2 $1.00

VOLPONE, Ben Jonson. 112pp. 28049-7 $1.00

DUBLINERS, James Joyce. 160pp. 26870-5 $1.00

A PORTRAIT OF THE ARTIST AS A YOUNG MAN, James Joyce. 192pp. 28050-0 $2.00

LYRIC POEMS, John Keats. 80pp. 26871-3 $1.00

THE BOOK OF PSALMS, King James Bible. 144pp. 27541-8 $1.00

DOVER·THRIFT·EDITIONS

Renascence
and
Other Poems

EDNA ST. VINCENT MILLAY

DOVER PUBLICATIONS, INC.
New York

DOVER THRIFT EDITIONS
Editor: Stanley Appelbaum

This Dover edition, first published in 1991, is an unabridged republication of the first edition, originally published by Mitchell Kennerley, New York, in 1917. Added in the Dover edition are a new Note and alphabetical lists of titles and first lines.

Manufactured in the United States of America
Dover Publications, Inc.
31 East 2nd Street
Mineola, N.Y. 11501

Library of Congress Cataloging-in-Publication Data

Millay, Edna St. Vincent, 1892–1950.
Renascence and other poems / Edna St. Vincent Millay.
    p.   cm. — (Dover thrift editions)
Includes indexes.
ISBN 0-486-26873-X (pbk.)
I. Title. II. Series.
PS3525.I495R4   1991
811'.52—dc20   91-11878
                                           CIP

Note

Renascence and Other Poems, of 1917, was the first volume of verse published by Edna St. Vincent Millay (1892–1950), American poet, short-story writer, playwright, librettist and actress. The title poem had been printed separately as early as 1912. The sonnet, of which six examples are included here, later became the verse form most closely associated with Millay. She was to win a Pulitzer Prize for poetry in 1923.

Although in the 1920s she was popularly regarded as a cynic, rebel and liberated woman, the simple and direct early works gathered in *Renascence and Other Poems* are more concerned with bereavement and sorrow, alleviated by a love of nature and a continuing search for happiness.

Contents

	PAGE
Renascence	1
Interim	9
The Suicide	17
God's World	23
Afternoon on a Hill	24
Sorrow	25
Tavern	26
Ashes of Life	27
The Little Ghost	28
Kin to Sorrow	30
Three Songs of Shattering	31
The Shroud	33
The Dream	34
Indifference	35
Witch-Wife	36
Blight	37
When the Year Grows Old	39
Sonnets I–V [Unnamed]	41
Sonnet VI [Bluebeard]	44

Renascence
and
Other Poems

Renascence

All I could see from where I stood
Was three long mountains and a wood;
I turned and looked another way,
And saw three islands in a bay.
So with my eyes I traced the line
Of the horizon, thin and fine,
Straight around till I was come
Back to where I'd started from;
And all I saw from where I stood
Was three long mountains and a wood.
Over these things I could not see;
These were the things that bounded me;
And I could touch them with my hand,
Almost, I thought, from where I stand.
And all at once things seemed so small
My breath came short, and scarce at all.
But, sure, the sky is big, I said;
Miles and miles above my head;
So here upon my back I'll lie
And look my fill into the sky.
And so I looked, and, after all,
The sky was not so very tall.
The sky, I said, must somewhere stop,
And—sure enough!—I see the top!

The sky, I thought, is not so grand;
I 'most could touch it with my hand!
And reaching up my hand to try,
I screamed to feel it touch the sky.
I screamed, and—lo!—Infinity
Came down and settled over me;
Forced back my scream into my chest,
Bent back my arm upon my breast,
And, pressing of the Undefined
The definition on my mind,
Held up before my eyes a glass
Through which my shrinking sight did pass
Until it seemed I must behold
Immensity made manifold;
Whispered to me a word whose sound
Deafened the air for worlds around,
And brought unmuffled to my ears
The gossiping of friendly spheres,
The creaking of the tented sky,
The ticking of Eternity.
I saw and heard, and knew at last
The How and Why of all things, past,
And present, and forevermore.
The Universe, cleft to the core,
Lay open to my probing sense
That, sick'ning, I would fain pluck thence
But could not,—nay! But needs must suck
At the great wound, and could not pluck
My lips away till I had drawn

All venom out.—Ah, fearful pawn!
For my omniscience paid I toll
In infinite remorse of soul.
All sin was of my sinning, all
Atoning mine, and mine the gall
Of all regret. Mine was the weight
Of every brooded wrong, the hate
That stood behind each envious thrust,
Mine every greed, mine every lust.
And all the while for every grief,
Each suffering, I craved relief
With individual desire,—
Craved all in vain! And felt fierce fire
About a thousand people crawl;
Perished with each,—then mourned for all!
A man was starving in Capri;
He moved his eyes and looked at me;
I felt his gaze, I heard his moan,
And knew his hunger as my own.
I saw at sea a great fog bank
Between two ships that struck and sank;
A thousand screams the heavens smote;
And every scream tore through my throat.
No hurt I did not feel, no death
That was not mine; mine each last breath
That, crying, met an answering cry
From the compassion that was I.
All suffering mine, and mine its rod;
Mine, pity like the pity of God.

Ah, awful weight! Infinity
Pressed down upon the finite Me!
My anguished spirit, like a bird,
Beating against my lips I heard;
Yet lay the weight so close about
There was no room for it without.
And so beneath the weight lay I
And suffered death, but could not die.

Long had I lain thus, craving death,
When quietly the earth beneath
Gave way, and inch by inch, so great
At last had grown the crushing weight,
Into the earth I sank till I
Full six feet under ground did lie,
And sank no more,—there is no weight
Can follow here, however great.
From off my breast I felt it roll,
And as it went my tortured soul
Burst forth and fled in such a gust
That all about me swirled the dust.

Deep in the earth I rested now;
Cool is its hand upon the brow
And soft its breast beneath the head
Of one who is so gladly dead.
And all at once, and over all
The pitying rain began to fall;
I lay and heard each pattering hoof

Upon my lowly, thatchèd roof,
And seemed to love the sound far more
Than ever I had done before.
For rain it hath a friendly sound
To one who's six feet underground;
And scarce the friendly voice or face:
A grave is such a quiet place.

The rain, I said, is kind to come
And speak to me in my new home.
I would I were alive again
To kiss the fingers of the rain,
To drink into my eyes the shine
Of every slanting silver line,
To catch the freshened, fragrant breeze
From drenched and dripping apple-trees.
For soon the shower will be done,
And then the broad face of the sun
Will laugh above the rain-soaked earth
Until the world with answering mirth
Shakes joyously, and each round drop
Rolls, twinkling, from its grass-blade top.
How can I bear it; buried here,
While overhead the sky grows clear
And blue again after the storm?
O, multi-colored, multiform,
Beloved beauty over me,
That I shall never, never see
Again! Spring-silver, autumn-gold,

That I shall never more behold!
Sleeping your myriad magics through,
Close-sepulchred away from you!
O God, I cried, give me new birth,
And put me back upon the earth!
Upset each cloud's gigantic gourd
And let the heavy rain, down-poured
In one big torrent, set me free,
Washing my grave away from me!

I ceased; and through the breathless hush
That answered me, the far-off rush
Of herald wings came whispering
Like music down the vibrant string
Of my ascending prayer, and—crash!
Before the wild wind's whistling lash
The startled storm-clouds reared on high
And plunged in terror down the sky,
And the big rain in one black wave
Fell from the sky and struck my grave.
I know not how such things can be;
I only know there came to me
A fragrance such as never clings
To aught save happy living things;
A sound as of some joyous elf
Singing sweet songs to please himself,
And, through and over everything,
A sense of glad awakening.
The grass, a-tiptoe at my ear,

Whispering to me I could hear;
I felt the rain's cool finger-tips
Brushed tenderly across my lips,
Laid gently on my sealèd sight,
And all at once the heavy night
Fell from my eyes and I could see,—
A drenched and dripping apple-tree,
A last long line of silver rain,
A sky grown clear and blue again.
And as I looked a quickening gust
Of wind blew up to me and thrust
Into my face a miracle
Of orchard-breath, and with the smell,—
I know not how such things can be!—
I breathed my soul back into me.
Ah! Up then from the ground sprang I
And hailed the earth with such a cry
As is not heard save from a man
Who has been dead, and lives again.
About the trees my arms I wound;
Like one gone mad I hugged the ground;
I raised my quivering arms on high;
I laughed and laughed into the sky,
Till at my throat a strangling sob
Caught fiercely, and a great heart-throb
Sent instant tears into my eyes;
O God, I cried, no dark disguise
Can e'er hereafter hide from me
Thy radiant identity!

Thou canst not move across the grass
But my quick eyes will see Thee pass,
Nor speak, however silently,
But my hushed voice will answer Thee.
I know the path that tells Thy way
Through the cool eve of every day;
God, I can push the grass apart
And lay my finger on Thy heart!

The world stands out on either side
No wider than the heart is wide;
Above the world is stretched the sky,—
No higher than the soul is high.
The heart can push the sea and land
Farther away on either hand;
The soul can split the sky in two,
And let the face of God shine through.
But East and West will pinch the heart
That can not keep them pushed apart;
And he whose soul is flat—the sky
Will cave in on him by and by.

Interim

The room is full of you!—As I came in
And closed the door behind me, all at once
A something in the air, intangible,
Yet stiff with meaning, struck my senses sick!—

Sharp, unfamiliar odors have destroyed
Each other room's dear personality.
The heavy scent of damp, funereal flowers,—
The very essence, hush-distilled, of Death—
Has strangled that habitual breath of home
Whose expiration leaves all houses dead;
And wheresoe'er I look is hideous change.
Save here. Here 'twas as if a weed-choked gate
Had opened at my touch, and I had stepped
Into some long-forgot, enchanted, strange,
Sweet garden of a thousand years ago
And suddenly thought, "I have been here before!"

You are not here. I know that you are gone,
And will not ever enter here again.
And yet it seems to me, if I should speak,
Your silent step must wake across the hall;
If I should turn my head, that your sweet eyes
Would kiss me from the door.—So short a time

To teach my life its transposition to
This difficult and unaccustomed key!—
The room is as you left it; your last touch—
A thoughtless pressure, knowing not itself
As saintly—hallows now each simple thing;
Hallows and glorifies, and glows between
The dust's grey fingers like a shielded light.

There is your book, just as you laid it down,
Face to the table,—I cannot believe
That you are gone!—Just then it seemed to me
You must be here. I almost laughed to think
How like reality the dream had been;
Yet knew before I laughed, and so was still.
That book, outspread, just as you laid it down!
Perhaps you thought, "I wonder what comes next,
And whether this or this will be the end";
So rose, and left it, thinking to return.

Perhaps that chair, when you arose and passed
Out of the room, rocked silently a while
Ere it again was still. When you were gone
Forever from the room, perhaps that chair,
Stirred by your movement, rocked a little while,
Silently, to and fro . . .

And here are the last words your fingers wrote,
Scrawled in broad characters across a page
In this brown book I gave you. Here your hand,
Guiding your rapid pen, moved up and down.

Here with a looping knot you crossed a "t,"
And here another like it, just beyond
These two eccentric "e's." You were so small,
And wrote so brave a hand!
                            How strange it seems
That of all words these are the words you chose!
And yet a simple choice; you did not know
You would not write again. If you had known—
But then, it does not matter,—and indeed
If you had known there was so little time
You would have dropped your pen and come to me
And this page would be empty, and some phrase
Other than this would hold my wonder now.
Yet, since you could not know, and it befell
That these are the last words your fingers wrote,
There is a dignity some might not see
In this, "I picked the first sweet-pea to-day."
To-day! Was there an opening bud beside it
You left until to-morrow?—O my love,
The things that withered,—and you came not back!
That day you filled this circle of my arms
That now is empty. (O my empty life!)
That day—that day you picked the first sweet-pea,—
And brought it in to show me! I recall
With terrible distinctness how the smell
Of your cool gardens drifted in with you.
I know, you held it up for me to see
And flushed because I looked not at the flower,
But at your face; and when behind my look

You saw such unmistakable intent
You laughed and brushed your flower against my lips.
(You were the fairest thing God ever made,
I think.) And then your hands above my heart
Drew down its stem into a fastening,
And while your head was bent I kissed your hair.
I wonder if you knew. (Beloved hands!
Somehow I cannot seem to see them still.
Somehow I cannot seem to see the dust
In your bright hair.) What is the need of Heaven
When earth can be so sweet?—If only God
Had let us love,—and show the world the way!
Strange cancellings must ink th' eternal books
When love-crossed-out will bring the answer right!
That first sweet-pea! I wonder where it is.
It seems to me I laid it down somewhere,
And yet,—I am not sure. I am not sure,
Even, if it was white or pink; for then
'Twas much like any other flower to me,
Save that it was the first. I did not know,
Then, that it was the last. If I had known—
But then, it does not matter. Strange how few,
After all's said and done, the things that are
Of moment.

    Few indeed! When I can make
Of ten small words a rope to hang the world!
"I had you and I have you now no more."
There, there it dangles,—where's the little truth
That can for long keep footing under that

When its slack syllables tighten to a thought?
Here, let me write it down! I wish to see
Just how a thing like that will look on paper!

"I had you and I have you now no more."

O little words, how can you run so straight
Across the page, beneath the weight you bear?
How can you fall apart, whom such a theme
Has bound together, and hereafter aid
In trivial expression, that have been
So hideously dignified?—Would God
That tearing you apart would tear the thread
I strung you on! Would God—O God, my mind
Stretches asunder on this merciless rack
Of imagery! O, let me sleep a while!
Would I could sleep, and wake to find me back
In that sweet summer afternoon with you.
Summer? 'Tis summer still by the calendar!
How easily could God, if He so willed,
Set back the world a little turn or two!
Correct its griefs, and bring its joys again!

We were so wholly one I had not thought
That we could die apart. I had not thought
That I could move,—and you be stiff and still!
That I could speak,—and you perforce be dumb!
I think our heart-strings were, like warp and woof
In some firm fabric, woven in and out;

Your golden filaments in fair design
Across my duller fibre. And to-day
The shining strip is rent; the exquisite
Fine pattern is destroyed; part of your heart
Aches in my breast; part of my heart lies chilled
In the damp earth with you. I have been torn
In two, and suffer for the rest of me.
What is my life to me? And what am I
To life,—a ship whose star has guttered out?
A Fear that in the deep night starts awake
Perpetually, to find its senses strained
Against the taut strings of the quivering air,
Awaiting the return of some dread chord?

Dark, Dark, is all I find for metaphor;
All else were contrast,—save that contrast's wall
Is down, and all opposed things flow together
Into a vast monotony, where night
And day, and frost and thaw, and death and life,
Are synonyms. What now—what now to me
Are all the jabbering birds and foolish flowers
That clutter up the world? You were my song!
Now, let discord scream! You were my flower!
Now let the world grow weeds! For I shall not
Plant things above your grave—(the common balm
Of the conventional woe for its own wound!)
Amid sensations rendered negative
By your elimination stands to-day,
Certain, unmixed, the element of grief;

I sorrow; and I shall not mock my truth
With travesties of suffering, nor seek
To effigy its incorporeal bulk
In little wry-faced images of woe.

I cannot call you back; and I desire
No utterance of my immaterial voice.
I cannot even turn my face this way
Or that, and say, "My face is turned to you";
I know not where you are, I do not know
If Heaven hold you or if earth transmute,
Body and soul, you into earth again;
But this I know:—not for one second's space
Shall I insult my sight with visionings
Such as the credulous crowd so eager-eyed
Beholds, self-conjured, in the empty air.
Let the world wail! Let drip its easy tears!
My sorrow shall be dumb!

—What do I say?
God! God!—God pity me! Am I gone mad
That I should spit upon a rosary?
Am I become so shrunken? Would to God
I too might feel that frenzied faith whose touch
Makes temporal the most enduring grief;
Though it must walk a while, as is its wont,
With wild lamenting! Would I too might weep
Where weeps the world and hangs its piteous wreaths
For its new dead! Not Truth, but Faith, it is

That keeps the world alive. If all at once
Faith were to slacken,—that unconscious faith
Which must, I know, yet be the corner-stone
Of all believing,—birds now flying fearless
Across would drop in terror to the earth;
Fishes would drown; and the all-governing reins
Would tangle in the frantic hands of God
And the worlds gallop headlong to destruction!

O God, I see it now, and my sick brain
Staggers and swoons! How often over me
Flashes this breathlessness of sudden sight
In which I see the universe unrolled
Before me like a scroll and read thereon
Chaos and Doom, where helpless planets whirl
Dizzily round and round and round and round,
Like tops across a table, gathering speed
With every spin, to waver on the edge
One instant—looking over—and the next
To shudder and lurch forward out of sight—

  * * * * * *

Ah, I am worn out—I am wearied out—
It is too much—I am but flesh and blood,
And I must sleep. Though you were dead again,
I am but flesh and blood and I must sleep.

The Suicide

"Curse thee, Life, I will live with thee no more!
Thou hast mocked me, starved me, beat my body sore!
And all for a pledge that was not pledged by me,
I have kissed thy crust and eaten sparingly
That I might eat again, and met thy sneers
With deprecations, and thy blows with tears,—
Aye, from thy glutted lash, glad, crawled away,
As if spent passion were a holiday!
And now I go. Nor threat, nor easy vow
Of tardy kindness can avail thee now
With me, whence fear and faith alike are flown;
Lonely I came, and I depart alone,
And know not where nor unto whom I go;
But that thou canst not follow me I know."

Thus I to Life, and ceased; but through my brain
My thought ran still, until I spake again:

"Ah, but I go not as I came,—no trace
Is mine to bear away of that old grace
I brought! I have been heated in thy fires,
Bent by thy hands, fashioned to thy desires,
Thy mark is on me! I am not the same
Nor ever more shall be, as when I came.

Ashes am I of all that once I seemed.
In me all's sunk that leapt, and all that dreamed
Is wakeful for alarm,—oh, shame to thee,
For the ill change that thou hast wrought in me,
Who laugh no more nor lift my throat to sing!
Ah, Life, I would have been a pleasant thing
To have about the house when I was grown
If thou hadst left my little joys alone!
I asked of thee no favor save this one:
That thou wouldst leave me playing in the sun!
And this thou didst deny, calling my name
Insistently, until I rose and came.
I saw the sun no more.—It were not well
So long on these unpleasant thoughts to dwell,
Need I arise to-morrow and renew
Again my hated tasks, but I am through
With all things save my thoughts and this one night,
So that in truth I seem already quite
Free and remote from thee,—I feel no haste
And no reluctance to depart; I taste
Merely, with thoughtful mien, an unknown draught,
That in a little while I shall have quaffed."

Thus I to Life, and ceased, and slightly smiled,
Looking at nothing; and my thin dreams filed
Before me one by one till once again
I set new words unto an old refrain:

"Treasures thou hast that never have been mine!
Warm lights in many a secret chamber shine

Of thy gaunt house, and gusts of song have blown
Like blossoms out to me that sat alone!
And I have waited well for thee to show
If any share were mine,—and now I go!
Nothing I leave, and if I naught attain
I shall but come into mine own again!"
Thus I to Life, and ceased, and spake no more,
But turning, straightway, sought a certain door
In the rear wall. Heavy it was, and low
And dark,—a way by which none e'er would go
That other exit had, and never knock
Was heard thereat,—bearing a curious lock
Some chance had shown me fashioned faultily,
Whereof Life held content the useless key,
And great coarse hinges, thick and rough with rust,
Whose sudden voice across a silence must,
I knew, be harsh and horrible to hear,—
A strange door, ugly like a dwarf.—So near
I came I felt upon my feet the chill
Of acid wind creeping across the sill.
So stood longtime, till over me at last
Came weariness, and all things other passed
To make it room; the still night drifted deep
Like snow about me, and I longed for sleep.

But, suddenly, marking the morning hour,
Bayed the deep-throated bell within the tower!
Startled, I raised my head,—and with a shout
Laid hold upon the latch,—and was without.

* * * *

Ah, long-forgotten, well-remembered road,
Leading me back unto my old abode,
My father's house! There in the night I came,
And found them feasting, and all things the same
As they had been before. A splendour hung
Upon the walls, and such sweet songs were sung
As, echoing out of very long ago,
Had called me from the house of Life, I know.
So fair their raiment shone I looked in shame
On the unlovely garb in which I came;
Then straightway at my hesitancy mocked:
"It is my father's house!" I said and knocked;
And the door opened. To the shining crowd
Tattered and dark I entered, like a cloud,
Seeing no face but his; to him I crept,
And "Father!" I cried, and clasped his knees, and wept.
Ah, days of joy that followed! All alone
I wandered through the house. My own, my own,
My own to touch, my own to taste and smell,
All I had lacked so long and loved so well!
None shook me out of sleep, nor hushed my song,
Nor called me in from the sunlight all day long.

I know not when the wonder came to me
Of what my father's business might be,
And whither fared and on what errands bent
The tall and gracious messengers he sent.

Yet one day with no song from dawn till night
Wondering, I sat, and watched them out of sight.
And the next day I called; and on the third
Asked them if I might go,—but no one heard.
Then, sick with longing, I arose at last
And went unto my father,—in that vast
Chamber wherein he for so many years
Has sat, surrounded by his charts and spheres.
"Father," I said, "Father, I cannot play
The harp that thou didst give me, and all day
I sit in idleness, while to and fro
About me thy serene, grave servants go;
And I am weary of my lonely ease.
Better a perilous journey overseas
Away from thee, than this, the life I lead,
To sit all day in the sunshine like a weed
That grows to naught,—I love thee more than they
Who serve thee most; yet serve thee in no way.
Father, I beg of thee a little task
To dignify my days,—'tis all I ask
Forever, but forever, this denied,
I perish."
        "Child," my father's voice replied,
"All things thy fancy hath desired of me
Thou hast received. I have prepared for thee
Within my house a spacious chamber, where
Are delicate things to handle and to wear,
And all these things are thine. Dost thou love song?
My minstrels shall attend thee all day long.

Or sigh for flowers? My fairest gardens stand
Open as fields to thee on every hand.
And all thy days this word shall hold the same:
No pleasure shalt thou lack that thou shalt name.
But as for tasks—" he smiled, and shook his head;
"Thou hadst thy task, and laidst it by," he said.

God's World

O world, I cannot hold thee close enough!
   Thy winds, thy wide grey skies!
   Thy mists, that roll and rise!
Thy woods, this autumn day, that ache and sag
And all but cry with colour! That gaunt crag
To crush! To lift the lean of that black bluff!
World, World, I cannot get thee close enough!

Long have I known a glory in it all,
       But never knew I this;
       Here such a passion is
As stretcheth me apart,—Lord, I do fear
Thou'st made the world too beautiful this year;
My soul is all but out of me,—let fall
No burning leaf; prithee, let no bird call.

Afternoon on a Hill

I will be the gladdest thing
    Under the sun!
I will touch a hundred flowers
    And not pick one.

I will look at cliffs and clouds
    With quiet eyes,
Watch the wind bow down the grass,
    And the grass rise.

And when lights begin to show
    Up from the town,
I will mark which must be mine,
    And then start down!

Sorrow

Sorrow like a ceaseless rain
    Beats upon my heart.
People twist and scream in pain,—
Dawn will find them still again;
This has neither wax nor wane,
    Neither stop nor start.

People dress and go to town;
    I sit in my chair.
All my thoughts are slow and brown:
Standing up or sitting down
Little matters, or what gown
    Or what shoes I wear.

Tavern

I'll keep a little tavern
   Below the high hill's crest,
Wherein all grey-eyed people
   May set them down and rest.

There shall be plates a-plenty,
   And mugs to melt the chill
Of all the grey-eyed people
   Who happen up the hill.

There sound will sleep the traveller,
   And dream his journey's end,
But I will rouse at midnight
   The falling fire to tend.

Aye, 'tis a curious fancy—
   But all the good I know
Was taught me out of two grey eyes
   A long time ago.

Ashes of Life

Love has gone and left me and the days are all alike;
   Eat I must, and sleep I will,—and would that night were
      here!
But ah!—to lie awake and hear the slow hours strike!
   Would that it were day again!—with twilight near!

Love has gone and left me and I don't know what to do;
   This or that or what you will is all the same to me;
But all the things that I begin I leave before I'm through,—
   There's little use in anything as far as I can see.

Love has gone and left me,—and the neighbors knock and
      borrow,
   And life goes on forever like the gnawing of a mouse,—
And to-morrow and to-morrow and to-morrow and to-morrow
   There's this little street and this little house.

The Little Ghost

I knew her for a little ghost
   That in my garden walked;
The wall is high—higher than most—
   And the green gate was locked.

And yet I did not think of that
   Till after she was gone—
I knew her by the broad white hat,
   All ruffled, she had on.

By the dear ruffles round her feet,
   By her small hands that hung
In their lace mitts, austere and sweet,
   Her gown's white folds among.

I watched to see if she would stay,
   What she would do—and oh!
She looked as if she liked the way
   I let my garden grow!

She bent above my favourite mint
   With conscious garden grace,
She smiled and smiled—there was no hint
   Of sadness in her face.

She held her gown on either side
    To let her slippers show,
And up the walk she went with pride,
    The way great ladies go.

And where the wall is built in new
    And is of ivy bare
She paused—then opened and passed through
    A gate that once was there.

Kin to Sorrow

Am I kin to Sorrow,
    That so oft
Falls the knocker of my door—
    Neither loud nor soft,
But as long accustomed,
    Under Sorrow's hand?
Marigolds around the step
    And rosemary stand,
And then comes Sorrow—
    And what does Sorrow care
For the rosemary
    Or the marigolds there?
Am I kin to Sorrow?
    Are we kin?
That so oft upon my door—
    Oh, come in!

Three Songs of Shattering

I

The first rose on my rose-tree
 Budded, bloomed, and shattered,
During sad days when to me
 Nothing mattered.

Grief of grief has drained me clean;
 Still it seems a pity
No one saw,—it must have been
 Very pretty.

II

Let the little birds sing;
 Let the little lambs play;
Spring is here; and so 'tis spring;—
 But not in the old way!

I recall a place
 Where a plum-tree grew;
There you lifted up your face,
 And blossoms covered you.

If the little birds sing,
 And the little lambs play,

Spring is here; and so 'tis spring—
   But not in the old way!

III

All the dog-wood blossoms are underneath the tree!
   Ere spring was going—ah, spring is gone!
And there comes no summer to the like of you and me,—
   Blossom time is early, but no fruit sets on.

All the dog-wood blossoms are underneath the tree,
   Browned at the edges, turned in a day;
And I would with all my heart they trimmed a mound for me,
   And weeds were tall on all the paths that led that way!

The Shroud

Death, I say, my heart is bowed
    Unto thine,—O mother!
This red gown will make a shroud
    Good as any other!

(I, that would not wait to wear
    My own bridal things,
In a dress dark as my hair
    Made my answerings.

I, to-night, that till he came
    Could not, could not wait,
In a gown as bright as flame
    Held for them the gate.)

Death, I say, my heart is bowed
    Unto thine,—O mother!
This red gown will make a shroud
    Good as any other!

The Dream

Love, if I weep it will not matter,
    And if you laugh I shall not care;
Foolish am I to think about it,
    But it is good to feel you there.

Love, in my sleep I dreamed of waking,—
    White and awful the moonlight reached
Over the floor, and somewhere, somewhere,
    There was a shutter loose,—it screeched!

Swung in the wind,—and no wind blowing!—
    I was afraid, and turned to you,
Put out my hand to you for comfort,—
    And you were gone! Cold, cold as dew,

Under my hand the moonlight lay!
    Love, if you laugh I shall not care,
But if I weep it will not matter,—
    Ah, it is good to feel you there!

Indifference

I said,—for Love was laggard, O, Love was slow to come,—
   "I'll hear his step and know his step when I am warm in
     bed;
But I'll never leave my pillow, though there be some
   As would let him in—and take him in with tears!" I said.
I lay,—for Love was laggard, O, he came not until dawn,—
   I lay and listened for his step and could not get to sleep;
And he found me at my window with my big cloak on,
   All sorry with the tears some folks might weep!

Witch-Wife

She is neither pink nor pale,
   And she never will be all mine;
She learned her hands in a fairy-tale,
   And her mouth on a valentine.

She has more hair than she needs;
   In the sun 'tis a woe to me!
And her voice is a string of colored beads,
   Or steps leading into the sea.

She loves me all that she can,
   And her ways to my ways resign;
But she was not made for any man,
   And she never will be all mine.

Blight

Hard seeds of hate I planted
    That should by now be grown,—
Rough stalks, and from thick stamens
    A poisonous pollen blown,
And odors rank, unbreathable,
    From dark corollas thrown!

At dawn from my damp garden
    I shook the chilly dew;
The thin boughs locked behind me
    That sprang to let me through;
The blossoms slept,—I sought a place
    Where nothing lovely grew.

And there, when day was breaking,
    I knelt and looked around:
The light was near, the silence
    Was palpitant with sound;
I drew my hate from out my breast
    And thrust it in the ground.

Oh, ye so fiercely tended,
    Ye little seeds of hate!
I bent above your growing

Early and noon and late,
Yet are ye drooped and pitiful,—
    I cannot rear ye straight!

The sun seeks out my garden,
    No nook is left in shade,
No mist nor mold nor mildew
    Endures on any blade,
Sweet rain slants under every bough:
    Ye falter, and ye fade.

When the Year Grows Old

I cannot but remember
   When the year grows old—
October—November—
   How she disliked the cold!

She used to watch the swallows
   Go down across the sky,
And turn from the window
   With a little sharp sigh.

And often when the brown leaves
   Were brittle on the ground,
And the wind in the chimney
   Made a melancholy sound,

She had a look about her
   That I wish I could forget—
The look of a scared thing
   Sitting in a net!

Oh, beautiful at nightfall
   The soft spitting snow!
And beautiful the bare boughs
   Rubbing to and fro!

But the roaring of the fire,
   And the warmth of fur,
And the boiling of the kettle
   Were beautiful to her!

I cannot but remember
   When the year grows old—
October—November—
   How she disliked the cold!

Sonnets

I

Thou art not lovelier than lilacs,—no,
   Nor honeysuckle; thou art not more fair
   Than small white single poppies,—I can bear
Thy beauty; though I bend before thee, though
From left to right, not knowing where to go,
   I turn my troubled eyes, nor here nor there
   Find any refuge from thee, yet I swear
So has it been with mist,—with moonlight so.

Like him who day by day unto his draught
   Of delicate poison adds him one drop more
Till he may drink unharmed the death of ten,
Even so, inured to beauty, who have quaffed
   Each hour more deeply than the hour before,
I drink—and live—what has destroyed some men.

II

Time does not bring relief; you all have lied
   Who told me time would ease me of my pain!
   I miss him in the weeping of the rain;
I want him at the shrinking of the tide;
The old snows melt from every mountain-side,
   And last year's leaves are smoke in every lane;

But last year's bitter loving must remain
Heaped on my heart, and my old thoughts abide!

There are a hundred places where I fear
　To go,—so with his memory they brim!
And entering with relief some quiet place
Where never fell his foot or shone his face
I say, "There is no memory of him here!"
　And so stand stricken, so remembering him!

III

Mindful of you the sodden earth in spring,
　And all the flowers that in the springtime grow,
　And dusty roads, and thistles, and the slow
Rising of the round moon, all throats that sing
The summer through, and each departing wing,
　And all the nests that the bared branches show,
　And all winds that in any weather blow,
And all the storms that the four seasons bring.

You go no more on your exultant feet
　Up paths that only mist and morning knew,
Or watch the wind, or listen to the beat
　Of a bird's wings too high in air to view,—
But you were something more than young and sweet
　And fair,—and the long year remembers you.

IV

Not in this chamber only at my birth—
　When the long hours of that mysterious night

Were over, and the morning was in sight—
I cried, but in strange places, steppe and firth
I have not seen, through alien grief and mirth;
   And never shall one room contain me quite
   Who in so many rooms first saw the light,
Child of all mothers, native of the earth.

So is no warmth for me at any fire
   To-day, when the world's fire has burned so low;
I kneel, spending my breath in vain desire,
At that cold hearth which one time roared so strong,
And straighten back in weariness, and long
   To gather up my little gods and go.

V

If I should learn, in some quite casual way,
   That you were gone, not to return again—
Read from the back-page of a paper, say,
   Held by a neighbor in a subway train,
How at the corner of this avenue
   And such a street (so are the papers filled)
A hurrying man—who happened to be you—
   At noon to-day had happened to be killed,
I should not cry aloud—I could not cry
   Aloud, or wring my hands in such a place—
I should but watch the station lights rush by
   With a more careful interest on my face,
Or raise my eyes and read with greater care
Where to store furs and how to treat the hair.

VI

Bluebeard

This door you might not open, and you did;
    So enter now, and see for what slight thing
You are betrayed. . . . Here is no treasure hid,
    No cauldron, no clear crystal mirroring
The sought-for truth, no heads of women slain
    For greed like yours, no writhings of distress,
But only what you see. . . . Look yet again—
    An empty room, cobwebbed and comfortless.
Yet this alone out of my life I kept
    Unto myself, lest any know me quite;
And you did so profane me when you crept
    Unto the threshold of this room to-night
That I must never more behold your face.
    This now is yours. I seek another place.

Alphabetical Lists of Titles and First Lines

Alphabetical List of Titles

	PAGE
Afternoon on a Hill	24
Ashes of Life	27
Blight	37
Bluebeard	44
Dream, The	34
God's World	23
Indifference	35
Interim	9
Kin to Sorrow	30
Little Ghost, The	28
Renascence	1
Shroud, The	33
Sonnets	41–44
Sorrow	25
Suicide, The	17
Tavern	26
Three Songs of Shattering	31
When the Year Grows Old	39
Witch-Wife	36

Alphabetical List of First Lines

	PAGE
All I could see from where I stood	1
All the dog-wood blossoms are underneath the tree!	32
Am I kin to Sorrow	30
"Curse thee, Life, I will live with thee no more!"	17
Death, I say, my heart is bowed	33
Hard seeds of hate I planted	37
I cannot but remember	39
If I should learn, in some quite casual way	43
I knew her for a little ghost	28
I'll keep a little tavern	26
I said,—for Love was laggard, O, Love was slow to come,—	35
I will be the gladdest thing	24
Let the little birds sing	31
Love has gone and left me and the days are all alike	27
Love, if I weep it will not matter	34
Mindful of you the sodden earth in spring	42
Not in this chamber only at my birth—	42
O World, I cannot hold thee close enough!	23
She is neither pink nor pale	36
Sorrow like a ceaseless rain	25
The first rose on my rose-tree	31
The room is full of you!—As I came in	9
This door you might not open, and you did	44
Thou art not lovelier than lilacs,—no	41
Time does not bring relief; you all have lied	41

DOVER · THRIFT · EDITIONS

All books complete and unabridged. All 5³/₁₆" × 8¼", paperbound.
Just $1.00 each in U.S.A.

POETRY

BHAGAVADGITA, Bhagavadgita. 112pp. 27782-8

SONGS OF INNOCENCE AND SONGS OF EXPERIENCE, William Blake. 64pp. 27051-3

SONNETS FROM THE PORTUGUESE AND OTHER POEMS, Elizabeth Barrett Browning. 64pp. 27052-1

MY LAST DUCHESS AND OTHER POEMS, Robert Browning. 128pp. 27783-6

POEMS AND SONGS, Robert Burns. 96pp. 26863-2

SELECTED POEMS, George Gordon, Lord Byron. 112pp. 27784-4

THE RIME OF THE ANCIENT MARINER AND OTHER POEMS, Samuel Taylor Coleridge. 80pp. 27266-4

SELECTED POEMS, Emily Dickinson. 64pp. 26466-1

SELECTED POEMS, John Donne. 96pp. 27788-7

THE RUBÁIYÁT OF OMAR KHAYYÁM: FIRST AND FIFTH EDITIONS, Edward FitzGerald. 64pp. 26467-X

A BOY'S WILL AND NORTH OF BOSTON, Robert Frost. 112pp. (Available in U.S. only.) 26866-7

THE ROAD NOT TAKEN AND OTHER POEMS, Robert Frost. 64pp. (Available in U.S. only) 27550-7

A SHROPSHIRE LAD, A. E. Housman. 64pp. 26468-8

LYRIC POEMS, John Keats. 80pp. 26871-3

THE BOOK OF PSALMS, King James Bible. 128pp. 27541-8

GUNGA DIN AND OTHER FAVORITE POEMS, Rudyard Kipling. 80pp. 26471-8

THE CONGO AND OTHER POEMS, Vachel Lindsay. 96pp. 27272-9

FAVORITE POEMS, Henry Wadsworth Longfellow. 96pp. 27273-7

SPOON RIVER ANTHOLOGY, Edgar Lee Masters. 144pp. 27275-3

RENASCENCE AND OTHER POEMS, Edna St. Vincent Millay. 64pp. (Available in U.S. only.) 26873-X

SELECTED POEMS, John Milton. 128pp. 27554-X

THE RAVEN AND OTHER FAVORITE POEMS, Edgar Allan Poe. 64pp. 26685-0

THE SHOOTING OF DAN MCGREW AND OTHER POEMS, Robert Service. 96pp. 27556-6

COMPLETE SONGS FROM THE PLAYS, William Shakespeare. 80pp. 27801-8

COMPLETE SONNETS, William Shakespeare. 80pp. 26686-9

SELECTED POEMS, Percy Bysshe Shelley. 128pp. 27558-2

SELECTED POEMS, Alfred, Lord Tennyson. 112pp. 27282-6

CHRISTMAS CAROLS: COMPLETE VERSES, Shane Weller (ed.). 64pp. 27397-0

GREAT LOVE POEMS, Shane Weller (ed.). 128pp. 27284-2

SELECTED POEMS, Walt Whitman. 128pp. 26878-0

THE BALLAD OF READING GAOL AND OTHER POEMS, Oscar Wilde. 64pp. 27072-6

FAVORITE POEMS, William Wordsworth. 80pp. 27073-4

EARLY POEMS, William Butler Yeats. 128pp. 27808-5

DOVER·THRIFT·EDITIONS

All books complete and unabridged. All 5³⁄₁₆″ × 8¼″, paperbound.
Just $1.00 each in U.S.A.

FICTION

FLATLAND: A ROMANCE OF MANY DIMENSIONS, Edwin A. Abbott. 96pp. 27263-X
BEOWULF, Beowulf (trans. by R. K. Gordon). 64pp. 27264-8
ALICE'S ADVENTURES IN WONDERLAND, Lewis Carroll. 96pp. 27543-4
O PIONEERS!, Willa Cather. 128pp. 27785-2
FIVE GREAT SHORT STORIES, Anton Chekhov. 96pp. 26463-7
FAVORITE FATHER BROWN STORIES, G. K. Chesterton. 96pp. 27545-0
THE AWAKENING, Kate Chopin. 128pp. 27786-0
HEART OF DARKNESS, Joseph Conrad. 80pp. 26464-5
THE SECRET SHARER AND OTHER STORIES, Joseph Conrad. 128pp. 27546-9
THE OPEN BOAT AND OTHER STORIES, Stephen Crane. 128pp. 27547-7
THE RED BADGE OF COURAGE, Stephen Crane. 112pp. 26465-3
A CHRISTMAS CAROL, Charles Dickens. 80pp. 26865-9
NOTES FROM THE UNDERGROUND, Fyodor Dostoyevsky. 96pp. 27053-X
SIX GREAT SHERLOCK HOLMES STORIES, Sir Arthur Conan Doyle. 112pp. 27055-6
WHERE ANGELS FEAR TO TREAD, E. M. Forster. 128pp. (Available in U.S. only) 27791-7
THE OVERCOAT AND OTHER SHORT STORIES, Nikolai Gogol. 112pp. 27057-2
GREAT GHOST STORIES, John Grafton (ed.). 112pp. 27270-2
THE LUCK OF ROARING CAMP AND OTHER SHORT STORIES, Bret Harte. 96pp. 27271-0
YOUNG GOODMAN BROWN AND OTHER SHORT STORIES, Nathaniel Hawthorne. 128pp. 27060-2
THE GIFT OF THE MAGI AND OTHER SHORT STORIES, O. Henry. 96pp. 27061-0
THE NUTCRACKER AND THE GOLDEN POT, E. T. A. Hoffmann. 128pp. 27806-9
THE BEAST IN THE JUNGLE AND OTHER STORIES, Henry James. 128pp. 27552-3
THE TURN OF THE SCREW, Henry James. 96pp. 26684-2
DUBLINERS, James Joyce. 160pp. 26870-5
SELECTED SHORT STORIES, D. H. Lawrence. 128pp. 27794-1
GREEN TEA AND OTHER GHOST STORIES, J. Sheridan LeFanu. 96pp. 27795-X
THE CALL OF THE WILD, Jack London. 64pp. 26472-6
FIVE GREAT SHORT STORIES, Jack London. 96pp. 27063-7
WHITE FANG, Jack London. 160pp. 26968-X
THE NECKLACE AND OTHER SHORT STORIES, Guy de Maupassant. 128pp. 27064-5
BARTLEBY AND BENITO CERENO, Herman Melville. 112pp. 26473-4
THE GOLD-BUG AND OTHER TALES, Edgar Allan Poe. 128pp. 26875-6
THE STRANGE CASE OF DR. JEKYLL AND MR. HYDE, Robert Louis Stevenson. 64pp. 26688-5
TREASURE ISLAND, Robert Louis Stevenson. 160pp. 27559-0
THE KREUTZER SONATA AND OTHER SHORT STORIES, Leo Tolstoy. 144pp. 27805-0
THE MYSTERIOUS STRANGER AND OTHER STORIES, Mark Twain. 128pp. 27069-6

DOVER · THRIFT · EDITIONS

All books complete and unabridged. All 5³⁄₁₆″ × 8¼″, paperbound.
Just $1.00 each in U.S.A.

FICTION

CANDIDE, Voltaire (François-Marie Arouet). 112pp. 26689-3
THE INVISIBLE MAN, H. G. Wells. 112pp. (Available in U.S. only.) 27071-8
ETHAN FROME, Edith Wharton. 96pp. 26690-7
THE PICTURE OF DORIAN GRAY, Oscar Wilde. 192pp. 27807-7

NONFICTION

THE DEVIL'S DICTIONARY, Ambrose Bierce. 144pp. 27542-6
SELF-RELIANCE AND OTHER ESSAYS, Ralph Waldo Emerson. 128pp. 27790-9
GREAT SPEECHES, Abraham Lincoln. 112pp. 26872-1
THE PRINCE, Niccolò Machiavelli. 80pp. 27274-5
SYMPOSIUM AND PHAEDRUS, Plato. 96pp. 27798-4
THE TRIAL AND DEATH OF SOCRATES: FOUR DIALOGUES, Plato. 128pp. 27066-1
CIVIL DISOBEDIENCE AND OTHER ESSAYS, Henry David Thoreau. 96pp. 27563-9

PLAYS

THE CHERRY ORCHARD, Anton Chekhov. 64pp. 26682-6
THE THREE SISTERS, Anton Chekhov. 64pp. 27544-2
THE WAY OF THE WORLD, William Congreve. 80pp. 27787-9
MEDEA, Euripides. 64pp. 27548-5
THE MIKADO, William Schwenck Gilbert. 64pp. 27268-0
SHE STOOPS TO CONQUER, Oliver Goldsmith. 80pp. 26867-5
A DOLL'S HOUSE, Henrik Ibsen. 80pp. 27062-9
HEDDA GABLER, Henrik Ibsen. 80pp. 26469-6
THE MISANTHROPE, Molière. 64pp. 27065-3
HAMLET, William Shakespeare. 128pp. 27278-8
JULIUS CAESAR, William Shakespeare. 80pp. 26876-4
MACBETH, William Shakespeare. 96pp. 27802-6
A MIDSUMMER NIGHT'S DREAM, William Shakespeare. 80pp. 27067-X
ROMEO AND JULIET, William Shakespeare. 96pp. 27557-4
ARMS AND THE MAN, George Bernard Shaw. 80pp. (Available in U.S. only.) 26476-9
THE SCHOOL FOR SCANDAL, Richard Brinsley Sheridan. 96pp. 26687-7
ANTIGONE, Sophocles. 64pp. 27804-2
OEDIPUS REX, Sophocles. 64pp. 26877-2
MISS JULIE, August Strindberg. 64pp. 27281-8
THE PLAYBOY OF THE WESTERN WORLD AND RIDERS TO THE SEA, J. M. Synge. 80pp. 27562-0
THE IMPORTANCE OF BEING EARNEST, Oscar Wilde. 64pp. 26478-5

For a complete list of all the Thrift Editions series write for a free
Thrift Editions brochure (58457-7).